Lost Borders

Rural Life in the American West of Long Ago

By Mary Hunter Austin

To
Marion Burke
and the
Friends of a Long Year

PANTIANOS
CLASSICS

Published by Pantianos Classics

ISBN-13: 978-1-78987-564-5

First published in 1909

"He said 'I have *missed* you so.'"

Contents

Let's have done with stranger faces, let's be quit of staring eyes,
Let's go back across Mohave where the hills of Inyo rise.
There's a word we've lost between us we shall never hear again
In the mindless clang of engines where they bray the hearts of men.
Let's go seek it east of Kearsarge where the seven-mile shadows run,
From the great gray bulk of Williamson heaved up against the sun.

Let's go look, for Hassayampa, with your arm across my shoulders,
Through the cañons of lost rivers by the bone-white bleaching bowlders,
Through the scented glooming hollows where the gray wolf shadows flee -
Where from Sur to Ubhebe only you and I shall be;
And the Word - I cannot name it, but we'll learn its sweetest use
In the moonlit sandy reaches when the desert wind is loose.

There's a little creek in Inyo, singing by beyond the town,
Through the pink wild-almond tangle and the birches slim and brown,
Where all night we'll watch the star-beams in the shallow, open rills,
And the hot, bright moons of August skulking low along the hills;
And the Word will wake in Inyo - never printed in a page -
With the wind that wakes the morning on a thousand miles of sage.

Chapter One - The Land

WHEN the Paiute nations broke westward through the Sierra wall they cut off a remnant of the Shoshones, and forced them south as far as Death Valley and the borders of the Mojaves, they penned the Washoes in and around Tahoe, and passing between these two, established themselves along the snow-fed Sierra creeks. And this it was proper they should do, for the root of their name-word is Pah, meaning water, to distinguish them from their brothers the Utes of the Great Basin.

In time they passed quite through the saw-cut cañons by Kern and Kings rivers and possessed all the east slope of the San Joaquin, but chiefly they settled by small clans and family groups where the pines leave off and the sage begins and the desert abuts on the great Sierra fault. On the northeast they touched the extreme flanks of the Utes, and with them and the southerly tribes swept a wide arc about that region of mysterious desertness of which you shall presently hear more particularly.

The boundaries between the tribes and between the clans within the tribe were plainly established by natural landmarks - peaks, hillcrests, creeks, and chains of water-holes beginning at the foot of the Sierra and continuing eastward past the limit of endurable existence. Out there, a week's journey from everywhere, the land was not worth parcelling off, and the boundaries which should logically have been continued until they met the cañon of the Colorado ran out in foolish wastes of sand and inextricable disordered ranges. Here you have the significance of the Indian name for that country - Lost Borders. And you can always trust Indian names to express to you the largest truth about any district in the shortest phrases.

But there is more in the name than that. For law runs with the boundary, not beyond it; it is as fast to the given landmarks as a limpet to its scar on the rock. I am convinced most men make law for the comfortable feel of it, defining them to themselves; they shoulder along like blindworms, rearing against restrictions, turning the reward for security as climbing plants .to the warmth of a nearing wall. They pinch themselves with regulations to make sure of being sentient, and organize within organizations.

Out there, then, where the law and the landmarks fail together, the souls of little men fade out at the edges, leak from them as water from wooden pails warped asunder.

Out there where the borders of conscience break down, where there is no convention, and behavior is of little account except as it gets you your desire, almost anything might happen; does happen, in fact, though I shall have trouble making you believe it. Out there where the boundary of soul and sense is as faint as a trail in a sand-storm, I have seen things happen that I do not believe myself. That is what you are to expect in a country where the names mean something. Ubehebe, Pharanagat, Resting Springs, Dead Man's Gulch, Funeral Mountains - these beckon and allure. There is always a tang of reality about them like the smart of wood smoke to the eyes, that warns of neighboring fires.

Riding through by the known trails, the senses are obsessed by the coil of a huge and senseless monotony; straight, white, blinding, alkali flats, forsaken mesas; skimpy shrubs growing little and less, starved knees of hills sticking out above them; black clots of pines high upon rubbishy mountain -heads days and days of this, as if Nature herself had obscured the medium to escape you in her secret operations.

One might travel weeks on end and not come on any place or occasion whereby men may live, and drop suddenly into close hives of them digging, jostling, drinking, lusting, and rejoicing. Every story of that country is colored by the fashion of the life there, breaking up in swift, passionate intervals between long, dun stretches, like the land that out of hot sinks of desolation heaves up great bulks of granite ranges with opal shadows playing in their shining, snow-piled curves. Out there beyond the borders are the Shivering Dunes, heaps upon heaps of blinding sand all acrawl in the wind, drifting and reforming with a faint, stridulent rustle, and black, wall-sided box-cañons that give the stars at midday, scored over with picture-writings of a forgotten race. There are lakes there of a pellucid clearness like ice, closed over with man-deep crystals of pure salt. Long Tom Bassit told me a story of one of these which he had from a man who saw it. It was of an emigrant train all out of its reckoning, laboring in a long, hollow trough of desolation between waterless high ranges, arriving at such a closed salt-pit, too much spent to go around it and trusting the salt crust to hold under their racked wagons and starveling teams. But when they had come near the middle of the lake, the salt thinned out abruptly, and, the forward rank of the party breaking through, the bodies were caught under the saline slabs and not all of them recovered. There was a woman among them, and the Man-who-saw had cared - cared enough to go back years afterward, when, after successive oven-blast summers, the salt held solidly over all the lake, and he told Tom Bassit how, long before he reached the point, he saw the gleam of red in the woman's dress, and found her at last, lying on her side, sealed in the crystal, rising as ice rises to the surface of choked streams. Long Tom wished me to make a story of it. I did once at a dinner, but I never got through with it. There, about the time the candles began to burn their shades and red track of the light on the wine-glasses barred the cloth, with the white, disdainful shoulders and politely incredulous faces leaning through the smoke of cigarettes, it had a garish sound. Afterward I came across the proof of the affair in the records of the emigrant party, but I never tried telling it again.

That is why in all that follows I have set down what the Borderers thought and felt; for that you have a touchstone in your own heart, but I should get no credit with you if I were to tell what really became of Loring, and what happened to the man who went down into the moaning pit of Sand Mountain.

Curiously, in that country, you can get anybody to believe any sort of a tale that has gold in it, like the Lost Mine of Fisherman's Peak and the Duke o' Wild Rose. Young Woodin brought me a potsherd once from a kitchen-midden in Shoshone Land. It might have been, for antiquity, one of those Job scraped himself withal, but it was dotted all over with colors and specks of pure gold from the riverbed from which the sand and clay were scooped. Said he:

"You ought to find a story about this somewhere."

I was sore then about not getting myself believed in some elementary matters, such as that horned toads are not poisonous, and that Indians really have the bowels of compassion. Said I:

"I will do better than that, I will make a story."

We sat out a whole afternoon under the mulberry-tree, with the landscape disappearing in shimmering heat-waves around us, testing our story for likelihood and proving it. There was an Indian woman in the tale, not pretty, for they are mostly not that in life, and the earthenware pot, of course, and a lost river bedded with precious sand. Afterward my friend went to hold down some claims in the Coso country, and I north to the lake region where the red firs are, and we told the pot-of-gold story as often as we were permitted. One night when I had done with it, a stranger by our camp-fire said the thing was well known in his country. I said, "Where was that?"

"Coso," said he, and that was the first I had heard of my friend.

Next winter, at Lone Pine, a prospector from Panamint-way wanted to know if I had ever heard of the Indian-pot Mine which was lost out toward Pharump. I said I had a piece of the pot, which I showed him. Then I wrote the tale for a magazine of the sort that gets taken in camps and at miners' boarding-houses, and several men were at great pains to explain to me where my version varied from the accepted one of the hills. By this time, you understand, I had begun to believe the story myself. I had a spasm of conscience, though, when Tennessee told me that he thought he knew the very squaw of the story, and when the back of the winter was broken he meant to make a little "pasear" in search of the lost river. But Tennessee died before spring, and spared my confessing. Now it only needs that some one should find another sherd of the gold-besprinkled pot to fix the tale in the body of desert myths. Well - it had as much fact behind it as the Gunsight, and is more interesting than the Bryfogle, which began with the finding of a dead man, clothless as the desert dead mostly are, with a bag of nuggets clutched in his mummied hands.

First and last, accept no man s statement that he knows this Country of Lost Borders well. A great number having lost their lives in the process of proving where it is not safe to go, it is now possible to pass through much of the district by guide-posts and well-known water-holes, but the best part of it remains locked, inviolate, or at best known only to some far-straying Indian, sheepherder, or pocket hunter, whose account of it does not get into the reports of the Geological Survey. But a boast of knowledge is likely to prove as hollow as the little yellow gourds called apples of Death Valley.

Pure desertness clings along the pits of the long valleys and the form-less beds of vanished lakes. Every hill that lifts as high as the cloud-line has some trees upon it, and deer and bighorn to feed on the tall, tufted, bunch grass between the boulders. In the year when Tonopah, turning upon itself like a swarm, trickled prospectors all over that country from Hot Creek to the Armagosa, Indians brought me word that the men had camped so close about the water-holes that the bighorn died of thirst on the headlands, turned always in the last agony toward the man-infested springs.

That is as good a pointer as any if you go waterless in the country of Lost Borders: where you find cattle dropped, skeleton or skin dried, the heads almost invariably will be turned toward the places where water-holes should be. But no such reminders will fend men from its trails. This is chiefly, I am persuaded, because there is something incomprehensible to the man-mind in the concurrence of death and beauty. Shall the tender opal mist betray you? the airy depth of mountain blueness, the blazonry of painted wind-scoured buttes, the far peaks molten with the alpen glow, cooled by the rising of the velvet violet twilight tide, and the leagues and leagues of stars? As easy for a man to believe that a beautiful woman can be cruel. Mind you, it is men who go mostly into the desert, who love it past all reasonableness, slack their ambitions, cast off old usages, neglect their families because of the pulse and beat of a life laid bare to its thews and sinews. Their women hate with implicitness the life like the land, stretching interminably whity-brown, dim and shadowy blue hills that hem it, glimmering pale waters of mirage that creep and crawl about its edges. There was a woman once at Agua Hedionda - but you wouldn't believe that either.

If the desert were a woman, I know well what like she would be: deep-breasted, broad in the hips, tawny, with tawny hair, great masses of it lying smooth along her perfect curves, full lipped like a sphinx, but not heavy-lidded like one, eyes sane and steady as the polished jewel of her skies, such a countenance as should make men serve without desiring her, such a largeness to her mind as should make their sins of no account, passionate, but not necessitous, patient - and you could not move her, no, not if you had all the earth to give, so much as one tawny hair's-breadth beyond her own desires. If you cut very deeply into any soul that has the mark of the land upon it, you find such qualities as these - as I shall presently prove to you.

Chapter Two - The Hoodoo of the Minnietta

ALL the trails in this book begin at Lone Pine, winding east by south and east again, though you will look long without finding the places where things happened in them unless you are susceptible to those influences that contribute to the fixed belief of mining countries, that the hot essences of greed and hate and lust are absorbed, as it were, by the means that provoke them, and inhere in houses, lands, or stones to work mischief to the possessor. This is common in new and untamed lands where destinies are worked out in plain sight. Manuel de Borba could not persuade Narcisse Duplin to accept as a gift the knife with which he killed Mariana, and no miner acquainted with its hoodoo will have anything to do with the Minnietta.

It lies out in the stark, wide light, on the red flanks of Coso, a crumbling tunnel, a ruined smelter, and a row of sun-warped cabins under tall, skeleton-white cliffs; and no man in these days visits it of his own intention.

Antone discovered it in a forgotten year. No one knew his other name; at Panimint he was called Dutchy, after the use of mining camps, from which you gather that he might have been a German, a Swede, Norwegian, Dane, or even a Dutchman. He was a foreigner, very sick when he came to the hills, sicker when he left them, and he discovered the ledge in a three weeks' prospecting trip, from which he returned to Jake Hogan's cabin with his pockets full of ore, elate, penniless, and utterly overworn.

He talked it all out with Hogan, on into the night, with the candle guttering in a bottle and the winking specimens spread out on the table between them. The ore was heavy and dull, and had the greasy feel of richness. Antone promised himself great things between the pains of a racking cough. He talked on afterward in his bunk, maunderingly, as his fever rose, to which succeeded the stupor of exhaustion. That was why, three days later, not being able to attend to it himself, Antone asked Hogan to have the ore assayed and bring him the report. And the report was so little in the eye of his expectation that a week later, loathing the filthy cabin and the ill-cooked food, feeling death in his throat, all his thought toward home, Antone accepted the two hundred dollars which Hogan offered him for all right and interest in his claim. Hogan saw him off considerately on the Mojave stage, and immediately gathered his pack to set out for a certain gully faced by tall, white cliffs, where the outcrop was heavy and dull with a greasy feel. Within a month it was known in all Panimint and Coso and as far north as Cero Gordo that Jake Hogan had made a good strike at the Minnietta.

Long afterward, when rage had made him drunk, Hogan, as he cursed the Minnietta, his wickedness, as it were, an added poison to his curse, told how one night while Antone lay sick, when the assayer had given him the full count of the ore, amazed by its richness, he had walked long in the one street barred with blocks of light from the dance-houses roaring full of song, and the light of the furnaces glowing low and evilly along the ground, walking up and down and contriving how he might impose on Antone the report of some other assay, and how, when he had done so successfully, he had bought the claim for a song. That, said Hogan, when he cursed the men who had done him out of the Minnietta, was the sort of man he was, as much as to say, being a toad, he spat venom and was not to be trod upon. But at the time he must have thought more cheerfully of his offence.

Hogan organized a stock company to open the mine and build a smelter, and began to grow rich amazingly. Jigging burro trains went up and down with water; eighteen-mule freighters trailed in with supplies in a wake of tawny dust. Beflounced and fluttered women, last indubitable evidence of a prosperous camp, preened themselves in the cabins set askew under the white cliffs.

It is not given to every man to deal successfully with mining stock-companies. Hogan, prospecting a grub stake, and Hogan, owner of the Minnietta putting out its thousands a week, were much the same person. Because he was ignorant Hogan did not understand his stock-company when he had organized it, and because he had come into his property by stealth, feared to lose it by conspiracy. Before the end of the second year Hogan and the Minnietta Mining and Milling Company were taking away each other's characters openly in court.

Hogan got a judgment that gave him little less than half that he asked; contumaciously carried it to a higher court and got a reversal of judgment that gave him nothing at all. So at the last he went out of the Minnietta with little more than he had brought into it folly and shame, you understand, peering with painted faces from the little cabins under the cliff, had had their pickings of him and going, cursed it with fluency and all his might. Tunnel and shaft and winze, he cursed it, sheave and cross-cut, pulley and belt and blast and fall rope under the hoist, as he had made it he cursed it in every part. Those who heard him maintain that in the cursing of Hogan was wrought the Hoodoo of the Minnietta; but, in fact, it began in the fake assay which Hogan carried to Antone in his bed, a villany of which he despoiled himself in his cursing, with the wantonness by which a man, checked in an evil, reveals the iniquity in which he shaped it.

After that the Minnietta Mining and Milling Company was not uniformly prosperous; the price of silver went down, or the quality of the ore fell off, and there were months at a time when the mine was shut down while the directors settled their private squabbles. Now and then, and always at inopportune moments, the company had streaks of economy. In one of these they happened upon McKenna for superintendent, whose particular qualification was that he was cheap, and being no spender at the best of times, was not always careful to draw his salary at the end of the month. This is very bad business for a mining country, as McKenna came to know when the next shutdown found him with a salary some fifteen months in arrears. He said uncomplimentary things about the management, but did not unnecessarily harass the directors, because he held his job on half pay until work began again, all of which was still unpaid when the mine reopened with a small force in April.

By this time, you understand, the Minnietta Mining and Milling Company was in a rather bad way. When the ore was of high grade, or the price of silver went up a few points, it would work the mine at a profit; when neither of these things happened it ran at a loss, and McKenna was their chief creditor. All this time the flux of mining life slacked throughout that district, slacked and dribbled away down the trails of desolate gulches, poured off quick, as it had come, like the sudden rains that burst over those ranges, leaving it scarred with dump and shaft and track. Houses full of cheap, garish furniture of the camps warped apart in the sun, rabbits ran in and out of the sagging sills. Five days' desolation lay between the world and the Minnietta.

During the shut-down McKenna stayed and looked after the mine, he said because it owed him so much he could not afford to neglect it; but really because the desert had him, cat-like, between her paws. So he stayed on and tinkered about repairs for the mill and the smelter. After one such session he was observed to go about in the tumultuous silence of a man with a doubtful project, also he ceased to vex the management greatly about his arrears of salary. And that was about a year before the Minnietta was shut down altogether.

In the course of time, McKenna, as the chief creditor, brought suit, attached the property of the Company, and got a judgment by default. At that time he could have had the whole district on the same terms, for something had happened, or was about to happen, in some other quarter which made the value of silver to the ton about half the cost of working it. The first thing McKenna did when he came into possession was to rip up the smelter.

This was before the cyanide process was discovered, and the smelter was of the rudest description - and McKenna had repaired it. Four great bars of virgin silver, half the length of a man's body and of incredible thickness, he took out of it in the way of leakings. McKenna used it to put the property in working order. The thing which was about to happen in Germany, or Argentina, or wherever, had not happened, or if it had, not with the anticipated effect. Silver went up. McKenna looked to the management himself, grew sleek, and married a wife. But the Hoodoo worked.

In the second year Mrs. McKenna had a child, and it died. Did I say somewhere that women mostly hate the desert? Women, unless they have very large and simple souls, need cover; clothes, you know, and furniture, social observances to screen them, conventions to get behind; life when it leaps upon them, large and naked, shocks them into disorder. Mrs. McKenna, at the Minnietta, had the arm-long grave under the skeleton cliffs, and McKenna, with no screen to his commonness. Her mind travelled back and forth from these and down the gulch to a vista of treeless discolored hills. Finally, for very emptiness, it fixed upon McKenna's assistant. The assistant was also common, but he had a little veil of unfamiliarity - and Mrs. McKenna was the only woman within three days. I do not say that what happened wouldn't have happened without the Hoodoo, given the conditions, any woman, and the man; but it served to take McKenna's mind off the mine, and the Hoodoo cut in between. After a while Mrs. McKenna and the superintendent went out of the story by way of the Mojave stage, and McKenna, leaving the mine in charge of Jordan, whom he had promoted from his foreman's job to be superintendent, was supposed to have gone in search of his wife. Whether he found her, or if the Hoodoo stayed by him in the place where he had gone, nobody ever heard. I think myself it inheres where it was bred, in the hollow of the comfortless thick hills. He was, however, bound to lose the mine in some such case as he had got it.

Jordan was the man McKenna had to help him when he ripped up the smelter; he knew exactly how the Minnietta came into his employer's hands and thought well of it. In every mining camp there are men incurably unable to be lessoned by the logic of events. McKenna was certain not to come near the mine again; might reasonably wish to be quit of it. This he might have done profitably, except for the Hoodoo, for the grade of the ore was increasingly rich. Jordan, as a practical miner, was much about the tunnel, and being left to himself too much, had time for thought, and, as I have said, he was the sort of man who admired the sort of thing McKenna had done. Along in the early summer the direction of the work in the main gallery was altered at never so slight an angle, and in due course of time was boarded over.

Jordan reported to McKenna that as the main lead appeared to be nearly worked out, it would be better to put the mine on the market before the fact became generally known. Eventually this was done. The selling price was not large, but considering what McKenna thought he knew of the property, and what the purchasers tipped by Jordan did know, it was satisfactory to both parties. In some unexplained way the Minnietta came shortly into the hands of his former foreman, Dan Jordan, who ripped up the siding and uncovered a body of high-grade ore.

The Minnietta is a nearly horizontal vein in a crumbling country rock that necessitates timbering and an elaborate system of props and siding. The new owner had all the petty, fiddling ways of a man accustomed to days' wages. He bought second-hand timbers from abandoned mines, and took unnecessary risks in the matter of siding, and the men grumbled.

Jordan did not get on well with his men; he gave himself airs, and suspected an attempt to cry down his new dignities. He was swelled and sullen with pride of his prosperity. By this time the conviction of the Hoodoo was well abroad in that country, and men were few and fearful who could be hired to work in the Minnietta. When there was a good twenty thousand on the dump the men refused to go into the tunnel again until certain things were remedied. Jordan, who did not believe in it, cursed the Hoodoo, cursed the hands, and went down into the tunnel, trailing abuse behind him for the men who followed timorously far at his back.

"Better keep this side the cut, sir," said one of them, respectfully enough, "them props ain't no ways safe." Jordan kicked the prop scornfully for all answer and when the men, starting back from the sound of falling, dared to come up with him, they found him quite dead, his skull crushed, and buried under the crumbling rock.

After that the Minnietta passed in due course to Jordan's heirs, two families of cousins who knew nothing of silver mines except that they were supposed to be eminently desirable.

Now, as they had come into the property through no fault of theirs, if the Hoodoo were nothing more than the logical tendency of evildoing to draw to and consume the evil-doer, they should have been beyond its reach. This would have been the case if, as you suppose, the Hoodoo were a myth begotten of a series of fortuitous events. But you, between the church and the police, whose every emanation of the soul is shred to tatters by the yammering of kin and neighbor, what do you know of the great, silent spaces across which the voice of law and opinion reaches small as the rustle of blown sand? There the castings of a man's soul lie in whatever shape of hate and rage he threw them from him.

There are places in Lost Valley where in the early fifties emigrant trains went through - places so void of wind and jostling weather that the wheel tracks show upon the sand, plain from that single passing; other places where, as at the Minnietta, the reek of men's passions lies in the hollow desertness like an infection, as if every timber had absorbed mischief instead of moisture, and every bolt gives it off in lieu of rust.

If it were not so there is no reason why the heirs of Dan Jordan should have gone to law about it while the price of silver went down and down. They stripped themselves in litigation while the timbers sagged in the tunnel and the cuts choked with rubble. The ore on the dump, by no means worth twenty thousand by this time, went to a lawyer who had been a very decent sort until he became dissolute through prosperity and neglected his family. The battens of the mill, warped through successive summers, fell off, and the boards shrunk from each other and curled at the edges like the lips of men dead and sundried in the desert. But if they should come together, or the price of silver go up, say three points, unless they be able to charge the enterprise with some counter-passion of nobility or sacrifice, they stand a chance to prove, in their own persons, how the Hoodoo works.

It is curious, though, and if we considered it long enough would no doubt be terribly disconcerting, to see how little account, when it deals with men singly, the desert takes of nobility as we conceive it between the walls. Clear out beyond the Borders the only unforgivable offence is incompetence; and conscience, in as far as it is a hereditary prejudice in favor of a given line of behavior, is no sort of baggage to take into the wilderness, which has its own exigencies and occasions, and will not be lived in except upon its own conditions. The case of Saunders is in point.

Chapter Three - A Case of Conscience

SAUNDERS was an average Englishman with a lung complaint. He tried Ashfork, Arizona, and Indio, and Catalina. Then he drifted north through the San Jacinta mountains and found what he was looking for. Back in England he had left so many of the things a man wishes to go on with, that he bent himself with great seriousness to his cure. He bought a couple of pack-burros, a pair of cayaques, and a camp kit. With these, a Shakespeare, a prayer-book, and a copy of *Ingoldsby Legends,* he set out on foot to explore the coast of Lost Borders. The prayer-book he had from his mother; I believe he read it regularly night and morning, and the copy of *Ingoldsby Legends* he gave me in the second year of his exile. It happened about that time I was wanting the *Ingoldsby Legends,* three hundred miles from a library, and book money hard to come by. Now there is nearly always a copy of *Ingoldsby Legends* in the vicinity of an Englishman. Englishmen think them amusing, though I do not know why. So I asked my friend, the barkeeper at the Last Chance, to inquire for it of the next Englishman who hit the town. I had to write the name out plainly so the barkeeper could remember it. The first who came was an agent for a London mining syndicate, and he left an address of a book-shop where it could be bought. The next was a remittance man, and of course he hadn't anything. If he had he would have put it in soak. That means he would have put the book up for is value in bad drink, and I write it as a part of our legitimate speech, because it says so exactly what had occurred: that particular Englishman had put everything, including his honor and his immortal soul, in soak. And the third was Saunders. He was so delighted to find an appreciator of the *Ingoldsby Legends* in the wilderness, that he offered to come to the house and render the obscure passages, and that was the beginning of my knowing about what went on later at Ubehebe.

Saunders had drifted about from water-hole to water-hole, living hardily, breathing the driest, cleanest air, sleeping and waking with the ebb and flow of light that sets in a mighty current around the world. He went up in summer to the mountain heads under the foxtail pines, and back in winter to watch the wild almond bloom by Resting Springs. He saw the Medicine dance of the Shoshones, and hunted the bighorn on Funeral Mountains, and dropped a great many things out of his life without making himself unhappy. But he kept the conscience he had brought with him. Of course it was a man's conscience that allowed him to do a great many things that by the code and the commandments are as wrong as any others, but in the end the wilderness was too big for him, and forced him to a violation of what he called his sense of duty.

In the course of time, Saunders came to a range of purplish hills lying west from Lost Valley, because of its rounded, swelling, fair twin peaks called Ubehebe (Maiden's Breast). It is a good name. Saunders came there in the spring, when the land is lovely and alluring, soft with promise and austerely virgin. He lingered in and about its pleasant places until the month of the Deer-Star, and it was then, when he would come up a week's journey to Lone Pine, for supplies, he began to tell me about Turwhasé, the gray-eyed Shoshone. He thought I would be interested, and I was, though for more reasons than Saunders at first supposed. There is a story current and confirmed, I believe, by proper evidence, that a man of one of the emigrant trains that suffered so much, and went so far astray in the hell trap of Death Valley, wandering from his party in search of water, for want of which he was partly crazed, returned to them no more and was accounted dead. But wandering in the witless condition of great thirst, he was found by the Shoshones, and by them carried to their campody in the secret places of the hills. There, though he never rightly knew himself, he showed some skill and excellences of the white men, and for that, and for his loose wit, which was fearful to them, he was kept and reverenced as a Coyote-man and a Medicine-maker of strange and fitful powers. And at the end of fifteen years his friends found him and took him away. As witness of his sojourning, there is now and then born to the descendants of that campody a Shoshone with gray eyes.

When Saunders began to tell me about Turwhasé, I knew to what it must come, though it was not until his mother wrote me that I could take any notice of it. Some too solicitous person had written her that Saunders had become a squaw-man. She thought he had married Turwhasé, and would bring home a handful of little half-breeds to inherit the estate.

She never knew how near Saunders came to doing that very thing, nor to say truth did I when I wrote her that her son was not married, and that she had nothing to fear; but with the letter I was able to get out of Saunders as much as I did not already know of the story.

I suppose at bottom the things a man loves a woman for are pretty much the same, though it is only when he talks to you of a woman not of his own class that he is willing to tell you what those things are. Saunders loved Turwhasé: first, because he was lonely and had to love somebody; then because of the way the oval of her cheek melted into the chin, and for the lovely line that runs from the waist to the knee, and for her soft, bubbling laughter; and kept on loving her because she made him comfortable.

17

I suppose the white strain that persisted in her quickened her aptitude for white ways. Saunders taught her to cook. She was never weary nor afraid. She was never out of temper, except when she was jealous, and that was rather amusing. Saunders told me himself how she glowed and blossomed under his caress, and wept when he neglected her. He told me everything I had the courage to know. When a man has gone about the big wilderness with slow death and sure camping on his trail, there is not much worth talking about except the things that are. Turwhasé had the art to provoke tenderness and the wish to protect, and the primitive woman's capacity for making no demands upon it. And this, in fine, is how these women take our men from us, and why, at the last, they lose them.

If you ask whether we discussed the ethics of Saunders' situation - at first there didn't appear to be any. Turwhasé was as much married as if Church and State had witnessed it; as for

She Had Become a Plaything of Which He Was Extremely Fond

Saunders, society, life itself, had cast him off. He was unfit for work or marrying; being right-minded in regard to his lung complaint, he drank from no man's cup nor slept in any bed but his own. And if society had no use for him, how had it a right to say what he should do out there in the bloomy violet spaces at Maiden's Breast? Yet, at the last, the Englishman found, or thought he found, a moral issue.

Maiden's Breast - virgin land, clear sun, unsullied airs, Turwhasé. Isn't there a hint all through of the myth of the renewal of life in a virgin em-

brace? A great many myths come true in the big wilderness. Saunders went down to Los Angeles once in the year to a consulting physician to please his mother, not because he hoped for anything. He came back from one such journey looking like a sleepwalker newly awakened. He had been told that the diseased portion of his lung was all sloughed away, and if nothing happened to him in six months more of Ubehebe, he might go home! It was then Saunders' conscience began to trouble him, for by this time, you understand, Turwhasé had a child - a daughter, small and gold-colored and gray-eyed. By a trick of inheritance the eyes were like Saunders' mother's, and in the long idle summer she had become a plaything of which he was extremely fond. The mother, of course, was hopeless. She had never left off her blanket, and like all Indian women when they mature, had begun to grow fat. Oh, I *said* he had a man's conscience! Turwhasé must be left behind, but what to do about the daughter lay heavily on Saunders' mind.

It made an obstinate ripple in his complacency like a snag in the current of his thought, which set toward England. Out there by the water-holes, where he had expected to leave his bones, life had been of a simplicity that did not concern itself beyond the happy day. Now the old needs and desires awoke and cried in him, and along with them the old, obstinate Anglo-Saxon prejudice that makes a man responsible for his offspring. Saunders must have had a bad time of it with himself before he came to a decision that he must take the child to England. It would be hard on Turwhasé; if it came to that, it would be hard on him - there would be explanations. As matters stood he looked to make a very good marriage at home, and the half-breed child would be against him. All his life she would be against him. But then it was a question of duty. Duty is a potent fetish of Englishmen, but the wilderness has a word bigger than that. Just how Turwhasé took his decision about the child I never heard, but as I know Indian women, I suppose she must have taken it quietly at first, said no, and considered it done with; then, as she saw his purpose clear, sat wordless in her blanket, all its folds drawn forward as a sign of sullenness, her thick hair falling on either side to screen her grief; neither moved to attend him, nor ate nor slept; and at last broke under it and seemed to accept, put the child from her as though it was already not hers, and made no more of it.

If there was in this acquiescence a gleam in her gray eye that witnessed she had found the word, Saunders was not aware of it.

As to what he felt himself in regard to Turwhasé, I am equally uninformed. I've a notion, though, that men do not give themselves time to feel in such instances; they just get it over with. All I was told was, that when at last he felt himself strong for it, Saunders put the child before him on the horse - she was then about two years old - and set out from Ubehebe. He went all of one day down a long box cañon, where at times his knees scraped the walls on either side, and over the tortuous roots of the mountain blown bare of the sand. The evening of the next day saw the contour of the Maiden's Breast purpling in the east, fading at last in the blurred horizon. He rode all day on glittering pale sands and down steep and utterly barren barrancas. All through that riding something pricked between his shoulders, troubled his sleep with expectancy, haunted him with a suggestion of impossible espionage. The child babbled at first, or slept in his arm; he hugged it to him and forgot that its mother was a Shoshone. It cried in the night and began to refuse its food. Great tears of fatigue stood upon its cheeks; it shook with long, quivering sobs, crying silently as Indian children do when they are frightened. Saunders' arm ached with the weight of it; his heart with the perplexity. The little face looked up at him, hard with inscrutable savagery. When he came to the Inyo range and the beaten trail, he distrusted his judgment; his notion of rearing the child in England began to look ridiculous. By the time he had cleared the crest and saw the fields and orchards far below him, it appeared preposterous. And the hint of following hung like some pestiferous insect about his trail.

In all the wide, uninterrupted glare no speck as of a moving body swam within his gaze. By what locked and secret ways the presence kept pace with him, only the vultures hung high under the flaring heaven could have known.

At the hotel at Keeler that night he began to taste the bitterness he had chosen. Men, white men, mining men, mill superintendents, well-dressed, competent, looked at the brat which had Shoshone written plainly all over it, and looked away unsmiling; being gentlemen, they did not so much as look at one another. Saunders gave money to the women at the hotel to keep his daughter all night out of his sight. Riding next day toward Lone Pine between the fenced lands, farms and farmhouses, schools, a church, he began to understand that there was something more than mere irresponsibility in the way of desert-faring men who formed relations such as this and left them off with the land, as they left the clothes they wore there and its tricks of speech.

He was now four days from Ubehebe. The child slept little that night; sat up in bed, listened; would whisper its mother's name over and over, questioning, expectant; left off, still as a young quail, if Saunders moved or noticed it. It occurred to him that the child might die, which would be the best thing for it.

Coming out of his room in the early morning he stumbled over something soft in a blanket. It unrolled of itself and stood up Turwhasé! The

20

child gave a little leap in his arms and was still, pitifully, breathlessly still. The woman stretched out her own arms, her eyes were red and devouring.

"My baby!" she said. "Give it to me!" Without a word Saunders held it out to her. The little dark arms went around her neck, prehensile and clinging; the whole little body clung, the lines of the small face softened with a sigh of unutterable content. Turwhasé drew up her blanket and held it close.

"Mine!" she said, fiercely. "Mine, not yours!"

Saunders did not gainsay her; he drew out all the money he had and poured it in her bosom. Turwhasé laughed. With a flirt of her blanket she scattered the coins on the ground; she turned with dignity and began to walk desertward. You could see by the slope of the shoulders under the blanket and the swing of her hips, as she went, that she was all Indian.

Saunders reached down to me from the platform of the train that morning for a last goodby. He was looking very English, smug and freshly shaven.

"I am convinced," he said, "that it really wouldn't have done, you know." I believe he thought he had come to that conclusion by himself.

What I like most about the speech of the campody is that there are no confidences. When they talk there of the essential performances of life, it is because they are essential and therefore worth talking about. Only Heaven, who made my heart, knows why it should have become a pit, bottomless and insatiable for the husks of other people's experiences, as if it. were not, as I declare it, filled to the brim with the entertainment of its own affairs; as if its mere proximity were an advertisement for it, there must be always some one letting fall confidences as boys drop stones in wells, to listen afterward in some tale of mine for the faint, reverberating sound. But this is the mark of sophistication, that they always appear as confidences, always with that wistful back-stroke of the ego toward a personal distinction. "I don't know why I am telling you this - I shouldn't like to have you repeat it" - and then the heart loosening intimacy of speech and its conscious easement.

But in a campody it is possible to speak of the important operations of life without shamefacedness. Mid-afternoons of late fall and winter weather - for though you may speak to your brother man without curtailment, it is not well to do so in summer when the snakes are about, for the snakes are two-tongued and carry word to the gods, who, if they are to be of use to you, must not know too much of your affairs - in mid-afternoon then, when the women weave baskets and grind at the metate, and the men make nets and snares, there is good talk and much to be learned by it. Such times the sky is hard like polished turquoise set in the tawny matrix of the earth, the creek goes thinly over the stones, and the very waters of mirage are rolled back to some shut fountain in the skies; the *plump, plump!* of the metate beats on under the talk of the women like the comfortable pulse of not too insistent toil.

When Indian women talk together, and they are great gossips, three things will surely come to the surface in the course of the afternoon - children, marriage, and the ways of the whites. This last appears as a sort of pageant, which, though it is much of it sheer foolishness, is yet charged with a mysterious and compelling portent. They could never, for example, though they could give you any number of fascinating instances, get any rational explanation of the effect of their familiar clear space and desertness upon the white man adventuring in it. It was as if you had discovered in your parlor-furniture an inexplicable power of inciting your guest to strange behavior. And what in the conduct of men most interests women of the campody, or women anywhere for that matter, is their relation to women. If this, which appears to have rooted about the time the foundations of the earth were laid, is proved amenable to the lack of shade, scarcity of vegetation, and great spaces disinterested of men not these of course, but the Power moving nakedly in the room of these things it only goes to show that the relation is more incidental than we are disposed to think it. There is nothing in the weather and the distance between water-holes to affect a man's feeling for his children, as I have already explained to you in the case of Saunders and Mr. Wills. But there where the Borders run out, through all the talk of the women, white women, too, who get no better understanding of the thing they witness to, through the thin web of their lives moves the vast impersonal rivalry of desertness. But because of what I said in the beginning I can tell you no more of that than I had from Tiawa in the campody of Sacabuete, where there are no confidences.

Chapter Four - The Ploughed Lands

TIAWA came from a Shoshone camp of three wickiups somewhere between Toquina and Fish Lake Valley. When she was young and comely she had come out of that country at the heels of a white man, and wrestled with the wilderness for the love of Curly Gavin. Gavin had been swamper for Ike Mallory's eighteen-mule team, and when the news of rich strikes in the Ringold district made red flares like rockets on Mallory's horizon, he grub-staked Curly to go with Burke and Estes to prospect the Toquina. Gavin had a lot of reddish curls and a lot of good-nature and small vices; the rest of him was sheer grit. The party was out three weeks, made some fair prospects, and had a disagreement. As to that, there was never any clear account, only it became immensely important to Gavin's own mind that he should get back to Maverick and record the location of some claims before Burke and Estes had a chance at them. Accordingly he left the others at Mud Springs, and, with one day's ration of water, set out by what he believed to be a short cut for home; and he had never been loose in the wilderness before! It was spring of the year after a winter of strong rains, and a bloom on the world, all the air soft as shed petals. Every inch of the moon-white soil had a flower in it, purple or golden; mornings the light made a luminous mist about the long wands of the creosote, at noon it slid and shimmered on the slopes as the hills breathed evenly in sleep. It is as easy, I say, to believe that such a land could neglect men to their death, as for man to believe that a lovely woman can be unkind. Gavin, for one, did not believe it.

By noon of the second day he began to suspect he had missed the trail - by night he was sure of it, and thinking to behave very sensibly walked back by the stars to recover the lost landmarks. By that time his water was quite gone. There came a time soon after that when the one consuming desire of the man was to get shut of the whole affair, the swimming earth that swung and tilted about the pivot of his feet, the hell-bent sun, the tormenting thirst, the glare of the sand that ate into his eyes. He was horribly bored; he wanted the thing to quit, to let him rest.

"Have done, curse you!" he shouted to it. As if the land had heard

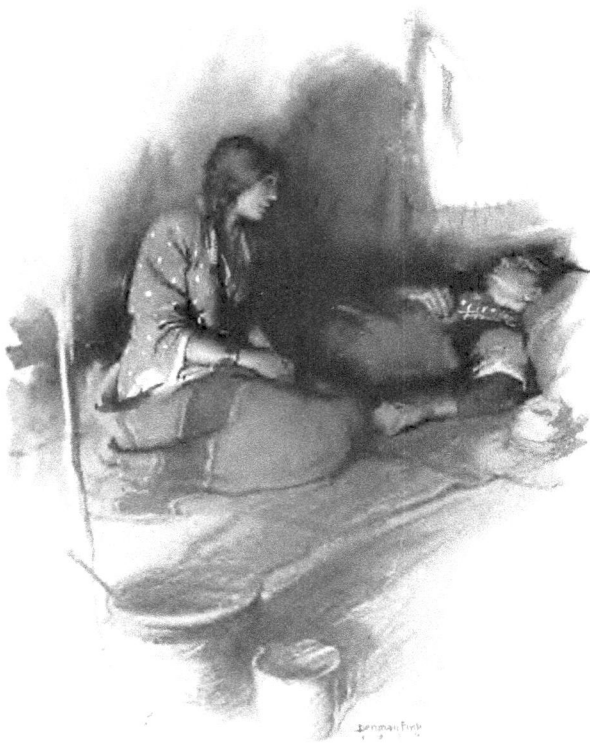

Before Gavin Was Quite Himself Again. Tiawa Tended Him

him, it reeled and sank; a grateful blackness swallowed all his sense. It

23

was about that time Tiawa's father, hunting chuckwallas, found him and led him to his camp.

In the interval before Gavin was quite himself again, Tiawa tended him. When he rose in his delirium to go to record those claims, she dropped her strong arms about him and eased him to the ground, rocking him in her bosom. So long as he did not know her, her tenderness had scope and power. But Gavin was annoyed when, as soon as he was able to travel, though not properly fit for it, he asked for a guide and got Tiawa. By the usage of her people it was Tiawa's right, because she loved him. She could do that these gentle savages who will not be seen walking abreast with their women grant them the right to love unasked and unashamed. *They* have no place, let me tell you, in the acceptance or rejection of a proffered love, for the snigger of the sophisticated male. Tiawa was pretty - so slim and round of limb, so smoothly brown and lustrous eyed! Gavin had no scruples, you may be sure; he was merely in the grip of another mistress who might or might not loose his bonds.

Well do I know the way of that tawny-throated one. If she but turns toward our valley with her hot breath to blow back the winter's rains, you hear the prophecy of that usurpation in the flat trumpeting of the bucks that bell the does; there will be few young that season in the lairs along Salt Creek, the quail will not mate; and this, mind you, if she no more than turns toward us her fulgent, her smiling for the three months between the harvest and the time of taboose. Judge, then what she would do to man.

Said Tiawa's father, who knew something of white men, and had looked between Gavin's eyes where the mark of the desert is set: "My daughter, when you have brought him as far as the ploughed lands, best you come home again."

Tiawa had put on her best bead necklace for the journey, and her cheeks were smooth with vermilion earth. She did not mean to come back. Tiawa told me this at Sacabuete, middle aged and fat, smiling above the metate as she paused in her grinding, for she had married a Paiute after Gavin left her, and made him very comfortable.

"But I did not know then," she said, "that a white man could take service from such as we and not requite it. If I had done the half of that for a Shoshone he would have loved me, for there were not two sticks laid together on that journey that I had not the doing of it."

They made a dry camp the first night, and when Gavin from sheer weakness lay down along the sand, and Tiawa had brought him food, before the glow was gone from the top of Toquina, when the evening star was lit and the heaven was clear and tender, he turned his back on Tiawa and stretched himself to sleep. On her side of the fire, Tiawa, dry-eyed and hot with shame, lay and pondered the reasons for these things. He was white, therefore he could accept her service without regarding the love that prompted it, and sleep upon it compunctionless. In the morning he spoke to her kindly, and she hoped again, for her desire was toward him and the spring was in her blood; but the obsession of his errand was on Gavin's mind, and he did not know. The morning wind blew out the strands of her thick hair, and shaped her garments to her loveliest curves as she brushed against him in the trail; every turn of her soft throat and the glint of her lustrous eyes was of love, but the sun-glare was heavy in his eyes, and he did not see. At the end of the third day, being at the end of her woman's devices, Tiawa bethought her of the gods. When it was full dark, before the moon was up, she went a little aside from the camp and made a medicine of songs. She swung and swayed to the postures of desire, beat upon the full, young, aching breast, and sang to the gods for the satisfaction of her love. Her voice reached him heavy with world-old anguish of women.

"Aw, shut up, can't you!" said Gavin. "I want to go to sleep!"

The desert had him. He had come into it fearlessly and unguarded, and it struck home; but Tiawa, who did not know any better, thought only that she had lost. She took off her bead collar because it had failed her, and wiped the vermilion from her cheeks. Only service remained, and that flowed from her as naturally as the long wands of the creosote flowed upon the wind. By day she went before him in the trails, by night at nameless water-holes she cooked his food. She did not know the places on the map where Gavin wished to go. She had set out by her father's direction for the shortest cut to the Ploughed Lands, and as they neared her heart sank inwardly as she remembered her father's word. For the Ploughed Lands meant the end of her Indian world. It meant white people, towns, farms at least - things, the desire of which had hurried Gavin mindlessly along the trail, the comfortable, long-turned furrow in which his life ran wontedly, the Ploughed Lands where he had no need of her.

Out here toward Toquina in the stark cañons, in the thin-sown pastures, she knew the way of subsistence; there in the fat, well-watered fields, unless Gavin accepted her when they came to the Ploughed Lands, she must go back. It is only our pitiful civilization, you understand, that attempts to magnify the love of man by shaming its end. In her own country Tiawa could venture much, as she pitted herself against the wilderness, but in the end she lay all night with her face between her arms weeping tearlessly. About noon of the last day they sighted the planted fields. From a hill-crest looking down they saw the dark smears of green on the golden valley, and out beyond these the line of willows, the thin gleam of the irrigating ditch like a blade from which the foiled desert started back. The rest of that day's trudging was down and down. Tiawa went before, and Gavin, breathing more evenly in the cooled air, felt the grip of the desert loosen on him with the tension of a spring released. He perceived suddenly that the woman was lovely and young. She was not so round by now, for they had come a long way with scant rations; but by the mark of her service upon her, he was suddenly aware that she loved him.

"Give me that pack," said Gavin; "you've carried it long enough."

The intent was kind, but to the girl it was the intimation of dismissal; he had refused her love, and now he would not even have her service. His tongue was freed of the spell of the silent places, and he talked as they went, pointing out this ranch and that as they went down.

About sunset they came to the out-curve of the canal and the farthest corner of an alfalfa field, and made their camp there. For the last time Tiawa laid the sticks together under the cooking-pot. For the last time; so it seemed to Tiawa. Lights began to come out in the ranch houses, faint and far. Tiawa thought of the little fires by the huts in Toquina; tears in her heart welled and brimmed about her eyes. Just then Gavin called her. She turned, and by the faint stars, by the dying flicker of their fire, she saw incredibly that he smiled. And to such as Tiawa, you understand, the smile of a white man - a man with ruddy curls, broad in the shoulders and young - is as the favor of the gods.

"Tiawa?"

"Great One!" she whispered.

Still smiling, he stretched out his arm to her and hollowed it in invitation ...for he had come to the Ploughed Lands. He was his own man again.

In the end - as I have already explained to you - Gavin went back to his own kind, and Tiawa married a Paiute and grew fat, for mostly in encounter with the primal forces woman gets the worst of it except now and then, when there are children in question, she becomes a primal force herself.

Great souls that go into the desert come out mystics - saints and prophets - declaring unutterable things: Buddha, Mahomet, and the Gallilean, convincing of the casual nature of human relations, because the desert itself has no use for the formal side of man's affairs. What need, then, of so much pawing over precedent and discoursing upon it, when the open country lies there, a sort of chemist's cup for resolving obligations? Say whether, when all decoration is eaten away, there remains any bond, and what you shall do about it.

Chapter Five - The Return of Mr. Wills

MRS. WILLS had lived seventeen years with Mr. Wills, and when he left her for three, those three were so much the best of her married life that she wished he had never come back. And the only real trouble with Mr. Wills was that he should never have moved West. Back East I suppose they breed such men because they need them, but they ought really to keep them there.

I am quite certain that when Mr. Wills was courting Mrs. Wills he parted his hair in the middle, and the breast-pocket of his best suit had a bright silk lining which Mr. Wills pulled up to simulate a silk handkerchief. Mrs. Wills had a certain draggled prettiness, and a way of tossing her head which came back to her after Mr. Wills left, which made you think she might have been the prettiest girl of her town. They were happy enough at first, when Mr. Wills was a grocery clerk, assistant Sunday-school superintendent, and they owned a cabinet organ and four little Willses. It might have been that Mr. Wills thought he could go right on being the same sort of a man in the West - he was clerk at the Bed Rock Emporium, and had brought the organ and the children; or it might have been at bottom he thought himself a very different sort of man, and meant to be it if he got a chance.

There is a sort of man bred up in close communities, like a cask, to whom the church, public opinion, the social note, are a sort of hoop to hold him in serviceable shape. Without these there are a good many ways of going to pieces. Mr. Wills' way was Lost Mines.

Being clerk at the Emporium, where miners and prospectors bought their supplies, he heard a lot of talk about mines, and was too new to it to understand that the man who has the most time to stop and talk about it has the least to do with mining. And of all he heard, the most fascinating to Mr. Wills, who was troubled with an imagination, was of the lost mines: incredibly rich ledges, touched and not found again. To go out into the unmapped hills on the mere chance of coming across something was, on the face of it, a risky business; but to look for a mine once located, sampled and proved, definitely situated in a particular mountain range or a certain cañon, had a smack of plausibility. Besides that, an ordinary prospect might or might not prove workable, but the lost mines were always amazingly rich. Of all the ways in the West for a man to go to pieces this is the most insidious. Out there beyond the towns the long Wilderness lies brooding, imperturbable; she puts out to adventurous minds glittering fragments of fortune or romance, like the lures men use to catch antelopes - clip! then she has them. If Mr. Wills had gambled or drank, his wife could have gone to the minister about it, his friends could have done something. There was a church in Maverick of twenty-seven members, and the Willses had brought letters to it, but except for the effect it had on Mrs. Wills, it would not be worth mentioning. Though he might never have found it out in the East, Mr. Wills belonged to the church, not because of what it meant to himself, but for what it meant to other people. Back East it had meant social standing, repute, moral impeccability. To other people in Maverick it meant a weakness which was excused in you so long as you did not talk about it. Mr. Wills did not, because there was so much else to talk about in connection with lost mines.

He began by grub-staking Pedro Ruiz to look for the Lost Ledge of Fisherman's Peak, and that was not so bad, for it had not been lost more than thirty years, the peak was not a hundred miles from Maverick, and, besides, I have a piece of the ore myself. Then he was bitten by the myth of the Gunsight, of which there was never anything more tangible than a dime's worth of virgin silver, picked up by a Jay hawker, hammered into a sight for a gun; and you had to take the gun on faith at that, for it and the man who owned it had quite disappeared; and afterward it was the Duke o' Wild Rose, which was never a mine at all, merely an arrow-mark on a map left by a penniless lodger found dead in a San Francisco hotel. Grub-staking is expensive, even to a clerk at the Bed Rock Emporium getting discounts on the grub, and grub-staked prospectors are about as dependable as the dreams they chase, often pure fakes, lying up at seldomvisited waterholes while the stake lasts, returning with wilder tales and clews more alluring. It was a late conviction that led Mr. Wills, when he put the last remnant of his means into the search for the White Cement mines, to resign his clerkship and go in charge of the expedition himself. There is no doubt whatever that there is a deposit of cement on Bald Mountain, with lumps of gold sticking out of it like plums in a pudding. It lies at the bottom of a small gulch near the middle fork of Owens River, and is overlaid by pumice. There is a camp kit buried somewhere near, and two skeletons. There is also an Indian in that vicinity who is thought to be able to point out the exact location - if he would. It is quite the sort of thing to appeal to the imagination of Mr. Wills, and he spent two years proving that he could not find it. After that he drifted out toward the Lee district to look for Lost Cabin mine, because a man who had immediate need of twenty dollars, had, for that amount, offered Wills some exact and unpublished information as to its location. By that time Wills' movements had ceased to interest anybody in Maverick. He could be got to believe anything about any sort of a prospect, providing it was lost.

The only visible mark left by all this was on Mrs. Wills. Everybody in a mining-town, except the minister and professional gamblers who wear frock-coats, dresses pretty much alike, and Wills very soon got to wear in his face the guileless, trustful fixity of the confirmed prospector. It seemed as if the desert had overshot him and struck at Mrs. Wills, and Richard Wills, Esther Wills, Benjy Wills, and the youngest Wills, who was called Mugsey. Desertness attacked the door-yard and the house; even the cabinet organ had a weathered look. During the time of the White Cement obsession the Wills family appeared to be in need of a grub-stake themselves. Mrs. Wills' eyes were like the eyes of trail-weary cattle; her hands grew to have that pitiful way of catching the front of her dress of the woman not so much a slattern as hopeless. It was when her husband went out after Lost Cabin she fell into the habit of sitting down to a cheap novel with the dishes unwashed, a sort of drugging of despair common among women of the camps. All this time Mr. Wills was drifting about from camp to camp of the desert borders, working when it could not be avoided, but mostly on long, fruitless trudges among the unmindful ranges. I do not know if the man was honest with himself; if he knew by this time that the clew of a lost mine was the baldest of excuses merely to be out and away from everything that savored of definiteness and responsibility. The fact was, the desert had got him. All the hoops were off the cask. The mind of Mr. Wills faded out at the edges like the desert horizon that melts in mists and mirages, and finally he went on an expedition from which he did not come back.

He had been gone nearly a year when Mrs. Wills gave up expecting him. She had grown so used to the bedraggled crawl of life that she might never have taken any notice of the disappearance of Mr. Wills had not the Emporium refused to make any more charges in his name. There had been a great many dry water-holes on the desert that year, and more than the usual complement of sun-dried corpses. In a general way this accounted for Mr. Wills, though nothing transpired of sufficient definiteness to justify Mrs. Wills in putting on a widow's dress, and, anyway, she could not have afforded it.

Mrs. Wills and the children went to work, and work was about the only thing in Maverick of which there was more than enough. It was a matter of a very few months when Mrs. Wills made the remarkable discovery that after the family bills were paid at the end of the month, there was a little over. A very little. Mrs. Wills had lived so long with the tradition that a husband is a natural provider that it took some months longer to realize that she not only did not need Mr. Wills, but got on better without him. This was about the time she was able to have the sitting-room repapered and put up lace curtains. And the next spring the children planted roses in the front yard. All up and down the wash of Salt Creek there were lean coyote mothers, and wild folk of every sort could have taught her that nature never makes the mistake of neglecting to make the child-bearer competent to provide. But Mrs. Wills had not been studying life in the lairs. She had most of her notions of it from the church and her parents, and all under the new sense of independence and power she had an ache of forlornness and neglect. As a matter of fact she filled out, grew stronger, had a spring in her walk. She was not pining for Mr. Wills; the desert had him - for whatever conceivable use, it was more than Mrs. Wills could put him to - let the desert keep what it had got.

It was in the third summer that she regained a certain air that made me think she must have been pretty when Mr. Wills married her. And no woman in a mining-town can so much as hint at prettiness without its being found out. Mrs. Wills had a good many prejudices left over from the time when Mr. Wills had been superintendent of the Sunday-school, and would not hear of divorce. Yet, as the slovenliness of despair fell away from her, as she held up her head and began to have company to tea, it is certain somebody would have broached it to her before the summer was over; but by that time Mr. Wills came back.

It happened that Benjy Wills, who was fourteen and driving the Bed Rock delivery wagon, had a runaway accident in which he had behaved very handsomely and gotten a fractured skull. News of it went by way of the local paper to Tonopah, and from there drifted south to the Funeral Mountains and the particular prospect that Mr. Wills was working on a grub-stake. He had come to that. Perhaps as much because he had found there was nothing in it, as from paternal anxiety, he came home the evening of the day the doctor had declared the boy out of danger.

It was my turn to sit up that night, I remember, and Mrs. Meyer, who had the turn before, was telling me about the medicines. There was a neighbor woman who had come in by the back door with a bowl of custard, and the doctor standing in the sitting-room with Mrs. Wills, when Mr. Wills came in through the black block of the doorway with his hand before his face to ward off the light - and perhaps some shamefacedness - who knows?

I saw Mrs. Wills quiver, and her hand went up to her bosom as if some one had struck her. I have seen horses start and check like that as they came over the Pass and the hot blast of the desert took them fairly. It was the stroke of desolation. I remember turning quickly at the doctor's curt signal to shut the door between the sitting-room and Benjy.

"Don't let the boy see you to-night, Wills," said the doctor, with no hint of a greeting; "he's not to be excited." With that he got himself off as quickly as possible, and the neighbor woman and I went out and sat on the back steps a long time, and tried to talk about everything but Mr. Wills. When I went in, at last, he was sitting in the Morris chair, which had come with soap-wrappers, explaining to Mrs. Meyer about the rich prospect he had left to come to his darling boy. But he did not get so much as a glimpse of his darling boy while I was in charge.

Mr. Wills settled on his family like a blight. For a man who has prospected lost mines to that extent is positively not good for anything else. It was not only as if the desert had sucked the life out of him and cast him back, but as if it would have Mrs. Wills in his room. As the weeks went on you could see a sort of dinginess creeping up from her dress to her hair and her face, and it spread to the house and the doorway. Mr. Wills had enjoyed the improved condition of his home, though he missed the point of it; his wife's cooking tasted good to him after miner's fare, and he was proud of his boys. He didn't want any more of the desert. Not he. "There's no place like home," said Mr. Wills, or something to that effect.

But he had brought the desert with him on his back. If it had been at any other time than when her mind was torn with anxiety for Benjy, Mrs. Wills might have made a fight against it. But the only practical way to separate the family from the blight was to divorce Mr. Wills, and the church to which Mrs. Wills belonged admitted divorce only in the event of there being another woman.

Mrs. Wills rose to the pitch of threatening, I believe, about the time Mr. Wills insisted on his right to control the earnings of his sons. But the minister called; the church put out its hand upon her poor, staggered soul that sunk aback. The minister himself was newly from the East, and did not understand that the desert is to be dealt with as a woman and a wanton; he was thinking of it as a place on the map. Therefore, he was not of the slightest use to Mrs. Wills, which did not prevent him from commanding her behavior. And the power of the wilderness lay like a wasting sickness on the home.

About that time Mrs. Wills took to novel-reading again; the eldest son drifted off up Tonopah way; and Benjy began to keep back a part of the wages he brought home. And Mr. Wills is beginning to collect misinformation about the exact locality where Peg-leg Smith is supposed to have found the sunburnt nuggets. He does not mention the matter often, being, as he says, done with mines; but whenever the Peg-leg comes up in talk I can see Mrs. Wills chirk up a little, her gaze wandering to the inscrutable grim spaces, not with the hate you might suppose, but with something like hope in her eye, as if she had guessed what I am certain of - that in time its insatiable spirit will reach out and take Mr. Wills again.

And this time, if I know Mrs. Wills, he will not come back.

Chapter Six - The Last Antelope

THERE were seven notches in the juniper by the Lone Tree Spring for the seven seasons that Little Pete had summered there, feeding his flocks in the hollow of the Ceriso. The first time of coming he had struck his axe into the trunk, meaning to make firewood, but thought better of it, and thereafter chipped it in sheer friendliness, as one claps an old acquaintance, for by the time the flock has worked up the treeless windy stretch from the Little Antelope to the Ceriso, even a lone juniper has a friendly look. And Little Pete was a friendly man, though shy of demeanor, so that with the best will in the world for wagging his tongue, he could scarcely pass the time of day with good countenance; the soul of a jolly companion with the front and bearing of one of his own sheep.

He loved his dogs as brothers; he was near akin to the wild things; he communed with the huddled hills, and held intercourse with the stars, saying things to them in his heart that his tongue stumbled over and refused. He knew his sheep by name, and had respect to signs and seasons; his lips moved softly as he walked, making no sound. Well what would you? a man must have fellowship in some sort.

Whoso goes a-shepherding in the desert hills comes to be at one with his companions, growing brutish or converting them. Little Pete humanized his sheep. He perceived lovable qualities in them, and differentiated the natures and dispositions of inanimate things.

Not much of this presented itself on slight acquaintance, for, in fact, he looked to be of rather less account than his own dogs. He was undersized and hairy, and had a roving eye; probably he washed once a year at the shearing as the sheep were washed. About his body he wore a twist of sheepskin with the wool outward, holding in place the tatters of his clothing. On hot days when he wreathed leaves about his head, and wove him a pent of twigs among the scrub in the middle of his flock, he looked a faun or some wood creature come out of pagan times, though no pagan, as was clearly shown by the medal of the Sacred Heart that hung on his hairy chest, worn open to all weathers. Where he went about sheep-camps and shearings there were sly laughter and tapping of foreheads, but those who kept the tale of his flocks spoke well of him and increased his wage.

Little Pete kept to the same round year by year, breaking away from La Liebre after the spring shearing, south around the foot of Pinos, swinging out to the desert in the wake of the quick, strong rains, thence to Little Antelope in July to drink a bottle for *La Quatorze,* and so to the Ceriso by the time the poppy fires were burned quite out and the quail trooped at noon about the tepid pools. The Ceriso is not properly mesa nor valley, but a long-healed crater miles wide, rimmed about with the jagged edge of the old cone.

It rises steeply from the tilted mesa, overlooked by Black Mountain, darkly red as the red cattle that graze among the honey-colored hills. These are blunt and rounded, tumbling all down from the great crater and the mesa edge toward the long, dim valley of Little Antelope. Its outward slope is confused with the outlines of the hills, tumuli of blind cones, and the old lava flow that breaks away from it by the west gap and the ravine of the spring; within, its walls are deeply guttered by the torrent of winter rains.

In its cup-like hollow, the sink of its waters, salt and bitter as all pools without an outlet, waxes and wanes within a wide margin of bleaching reeds. Nothing taller shows in all the Ceriso, and the wind among them fills all the hollow with an eerie whispering. One spring rills down by the gorge of an old flow on the side toward Little Antelope, and, but for the lone juniper that stood by it, there is never a tree until you come to the foot of Black Mountain.

The flock of Little Pete, a maverick strayed from some rodeo, a prospector going up to Black Mountain, and a solitary antelope were all that passed through the Ceriso at any time. The antelope had the best right. He came as of old habit; he had come when the lightfoot herds ranged from here to the sweet, mist-watered cañons of the Coast Range, and the bucks went up to the windy mesas what time the young ran with their mothers, nose to flank. They had ceased before the keen edge of slaughter that defines the frontier of men.

All that a tardy law had saved to the district of Little Antelope was the buck that came up the ravine of the Lone Tree Spring at the set time of the year when Little Pete fed his flock in the Ceriso, and Pete averred that they were glad to see each other. True enough, they were each the friendliest thing the other found there; for though the law ran as far as the antelope ranged, there were hill-dwellers who took no account of it - namely, the coyotes. They hunted the buck in season and out, bayed him down from the feeding grounds, fended him from the pool, pursued him by relay races, ambushed him in the pitfalls of the black rock.

There were seven coyotes ranging the east side of the Ceriso at the time when Little Pete first struck his axe into the juniper-tree, slinking, sly-footed, and evil-eyed. Many an evening the shepherd watched them running lightly in the hollow of the crater, the flash flash of the antelope's white rump signalling the progress of the chase. But always the buck outran or outwitted them, taking to the high, broken ridges where no split foot could follow his seven-leagued bounds. Many a morning Little Pete, tending his cooking-pot by a quavering sagebrush fire, saw the antelope feeding down toward the Lone Tree Spring, and looked his sentiments. The coyotes had spoken theirs all in the night with derisive voices; never was there any love lost between a shepherd and a coyote. The prong-horn's chief recommendation to an acquaintance was that he could outdo them.

After the third summer, Pete began to perceive a reciprocal friendliness in the antelope. Early mornings the shepherd saw him rising from his lair, or came often upon the warm pressed hollow where he had lain within cry of his coyote-scaring fire. When it was midday in the misty hollow and the shadows drawn close, stuck tight under the juniper and the sage, they went each to his nooning in his own fashion, but in the half light they drew near together.

Since the beginning of the law the antelope had half forgotten his fear of man. He looked upon the shepherd with steadfastness, he smelled the smell of his garments which was the smell of sheep and the unhandled earth, and the smell of wood smoke was in his hair. They had companion-ship without speech; they conferred favors silently after the manner of those who understand one another. The antelope led to the best feeding-grounds, and Pete kept the sheep from muddying the spring until the buck had drunk. When the coyotes skulked in the scrub by night to deride him, the shepherd mocked them in their own tongue, and promised them the best of his lambs for the killing; but to hear afar off their hunting howl stirred him out of sleep to curse with great heartiness. At such times he thought of the antelope and wished him well.

Beginning with the west gap opposite the Lone Tree Spring about the 1st of August, Pete would feed all around the broken rim of the crater, up the gullies and down, and clean through the hollow of it in a matter of two months, or if the winter had been a wet one, a little longer, and in seven years the man and the antelope grew to know each other very well. Where the flock fed the buck fed, keeping farthest from the dogs, and at last he came to lie down with it.

That was after a season of scant rains, when the feed was poor and the antelope's flank grew thin; the rabbits had trooped down to the irrigated lands, and the coyotes, made more keen by hunger, pressed him hard. One of those smoky, yawning days when the sky hugged the earth, and all sound fell back from a woolly atmosphere and broke dully in the scrub, about the usual hour of their running between twilight and mid-afternoon, the coyotes drove the tall buck, winded, desperate, and fore-done, to refuge among the silly sheep, where for fear of the dogs and the man the howlers dared not come. He stood at bay there, fronting the shepherd, brought up against a crisis greatly needing the help of speech.

34

Well - he had nearly as much gift in that matter as Little Pete. Those two silent ones understood each other; some assurance, the warrant of a free-given faith, passed between them. The buck lowered his head and eased the sharp throbbing of his ribs; the dogs drew in the scattered flocks; they moved, keeping a little cleared space nearest the buck; he moved with them; he began to feed. Thereafter the heart of Little Pete warmed humanly toward the antelope, and the coyotes began to be very personal in their abuse. That same night they drew off the shepherd's dogs by a ruse and stole two of his lambs.

The same seasons that made the friendliness of the antelope and Little Pete wore the face of the shepherd into a keener likeness to the weathered hills, and the juniper flourishing greenly by the spring bade fair to outlast them both. The line of ploughed lands stretched out mile by mile from the lower valley, and a solitary homesteader built him a cabin at the foot of the Ceriso.

In seven years a coyote may learn somewhat; those of the Ceriso learned the ways of Little Pete and the antelope. Trust them to have noted, as the years moved, that the buck's flanks were lean and his step less free. Put it that the antelope was old, and that he made truce with the shepherd to hide the failing of his powers; then if he came earlier or stayed later than the flock, it would go hard with him. But as if he knew their mind in the matter, the antelope delayed his coming until the salt pool shrunk to its innermost ring of reeds, and the sun-cured grasses crisped along the slope. It seemed the brute sense waked between him and the man to make each aware of the other's nearness. Often as Little Pete drove in by the west gap he would sight the prongs of the buck rising over the barrier of black rocks at the head of the ravine. Together they passed out of the crater, keeping fellowship as far as the frontier of evergreen oaks. Here Little Pete turned in by the cattle fences to come at La Liebre from the north, and the antelope, avoiding all man-trails, growing daily more remote, passed into the wooded hills on unguessed errands of his own.

Twice the homesteader saw the antelope go up to the Ceriso at that set time of the year. The third summer when he sighted him, a whitish speck moving steadily against the fawn-colored background of the hills, the homesteader took down his rifle and made haste into the crater. At that time his cabin stood on the remotest edge of settlement, and the grip of the law was loosened in so long a reach.

"In the end the coyotes will get him. Better that he fall to me," said the homesteader. But, in fact, he was prompted by the love of mastery, which for the most part moves men into new lands, whose creatures they conceive given over into their hands.

The coyote that kept the watch at the head of the ravine saw him come, and lifted up his voice in the long-drawn dolorous whine that warned the other watchers in their unseen stations in the scrub. The homesteader heard also, and let a curse softly under his breath, for besides that they might scare his quarry, he coveted the howler's ears, in which the law upheld him. Never a tip nor a tail of one showed above the sage when he had come up into the Ceriso.

The afternoon wore on; the homesteader hid in the reeds, and the coyotes had forgotten him. Away to the left in a windless blur of dust the sheep of Little Pete trailed up toward the crater's rim. The leader, watching by the spring, caught a jack-rabbit and was eating it quietly behind the black rock.

In the mean time the last antelope came lightly and securely by the gully, by the black rock and the lone juniper, into the Ceriso. The friendliness of the antelope for Little Pete betrayed him. He came with some sense of home, expecting the flock and protection of man-presence. He strayed witlessly into the open, his ears set to catch the jangle of the bells. What he heard was the snick of the breech-bolt as the homesteader threw up the sight of his rifle, and a small demoniac cry that ran from gutter to gutter of the crater rim, impossible to gauge for numbers or distance.

At that moment Little Pete worried the flock up the outward slope where the ruin of the old lava flows gave sharply back the wrangle of the bells. Three weeks he had won up from the Little Antelope, and three by way of the Sand Flat, where there was great scarcity of water, and in all that time none of his kind had hailed him. His heart warmed toward the juniper-tree and the antelope whose hoof-prints he found in the white dust of the mesa trail. Men had small respect by Little Pete, women he had no time for: the antelope was the noblest thing he had ever loved. The sheep poured through the gap and spread fanwise down the gully; behind them Little Pete twirled his staff, and made merry wordless noises in his throat in anticipation of friendliness. "Ehu!" he cried when he heard the hunting howl, "but they are at their tricks again," and then in English he voiced a volley of broken, inconsequential oaths, for he saw what the howlers were about.

One imputes a sixth sense to that son of a thief misnamed the coyote, to make up for speech - persuasion, concerted movement - in short, the human faculty. How else do they manage the terrible relay races by which they make quarry of the fleetest-footed? It was so they plotted the antelope's last running in the Ceriso: two to start the chase from the black rock toward the red scar of a winter torrent, two to leave the mouth of the wash when the first were winded, one to fend the ravine that led up to the broken ridges, one to start out of the scrub at the base of a smooth upward sweep, and, running parallel to it, keep the buck well into the open; all these when their first spurt was done to cross leisurely to new stations to take up another turn. Round they went in the hollow of the crater, velvet-footed and sly even in full chase, and biding their time. It was a good running, but it was almost done when away by the west gap the buck heard the voice of Little Pete raised in adjuration and the friendly blether of the sheep. Thin spirals of dust flared upward from the moving flocks and signalled truce to chase. He broke for it with wide panting bounds and many a missed step picked up with incredible eagerness, the thin rim of his nostrils oozing blood. The coyotes saw and closed in about him, chopping quick and hard. Sharp ears and sharp muzzles cast up at his throat, and were whelmed in a press of gray flanks. One yelped, one went limping from a kick, and one went past him, returning with a spring upon the heaving shoulder, and the man in the reeds beside the bitter water rose up and fired.

All the luck of that day's hunting went to the homesteader, for he had killed an antelope and a coyote with one shot, and though he had a bad quarter of an hour with a wild and loathly shepherd, who he feared might denounce him to the law, in the end he made off with the last antelope, swung limp and graceless across his shoulder. The coyotes came back to the killing-ground when they had watched him safely down the ravine, and were consoled with what they found. As they pulled the body of the dead leader about before they began upon it, they noticed that the homesteader had taken the ears of that also.

Little Pete lay in the grass and wept simply; the tears made pallid traces in the season's grime. He suffered the torture, the question extraordinary of bereavement. If he had not lingered so long in the meadow of Los Robles, if he had moved faster on the Sand Flat trail - but, in fact, he had come up against the inevitable. He had been breathed upon by that spirit which goes before cities like an exhalation and dries up the gossamer and the dew.

From that day the heart had gone out of the Ceriso. It was a desolate hollow, reddish-hued and dim, with brackish waters, and moreover the feed was poor. His eyes could not forget their trick of roving the valley at all hours; he looked by the rill of the spring for hoof-prints that were not there.

Fronting the west gap there was a spot where he would not feed, where the grass stood up stiff and black with what had dried upon it. He kept the flocks to the ridgy slopes where the limited horizon permitted one to believe the crater was not quite empty. His heart shook in the night to hear the long-drawn hunting howl, and shook again remembering that he had nothing to be fearing for. After three weeks he passed out on the other side and came that way no more. The juniper -tree stood greenly by the spring until the homesteader cut it down for firewood. Nothing taller than the rattling reeds stirs in all the hollow of the Ceriso.

There was a man once who skidded through Lost Borders in an automobile with a balloon silk tent and a folding tin bath-tub, who wrote some cheerful tales about that country, mostly untrue, about rattlesnakes coiling under men's blankets at night, to afford heroic occasions in the morning, of which circumstance seventeen years' residence failed to furnish a single instance; about lost mines rediscovered, which never happens, and Indian maidens of such surpassing charm that men married them and went out of the story with intimations of ever-after happiness due to arrive. It is true I did know a man who married his *mahala,* but he was mighty sorry for it, and though it lost him his chance in life the story is not worth telling.

The fact is that only when men struggle with men do you get triumphs and rejoicings. In any conflict with the immutable forces the human is always the under dog, and when the struggle is sharp enough to be dramatic, he wins death mostly; happiest if he gets out of it some dignity for himself and some sweetness for his friends to remember. I was a long time understanding why a great many people cannot abide a story with death in it. To be snatched at the dramatic moment, to be reabsorbed in the vastness of space and the infinitude of silences, to return simply to the native essences - that is nothing to make moan about; but when I had once taken part in a proper Christian funeral, after fifteen years without witnessing one such, I was less surprised at it.

When one has to think of death in connection with strange tiptoeing men felicitating themselves on millinery effects, with the suggestion of what was to be charged for it lurking under the discreetly dropped lids, and all the obvious mechanism of modern burial, one can understand that what happened at Agua Dulce is quite another matter.

Chapter Seven - Agua Dulce

THE Los Angeles special got in so late that day that if the driver of the Mojave stage had not, from having once gone to school to me, acquired the habit of minding what I said, I should never have made it. I hailed him from the station, and he swung the four about in the wide street as the wind swept me toward the racked old coach in a blinding whirl of dust.

It wrapped my skirts about the iron gear of the coach as I climbed to the seat beside the driver, and as we dropped the town behind us, lifted my hat and searched out my hairpins. But it was the desert wind, and the smell it carried was the smell of marrow-fat weed and gilias after the sun goes down; so, because I had been very unhappy away from it, and was now drunk with the joy of renewal, and as in my case there would be no time for a toilet proper to the road until we came to the Eighteen-mile house, I was satisfied merely to cling to the pitching front of the coach and let the wind do what it would. The sky was alight and saffron-tinted, the mountains bloomed with violet shadows; as we came whirling by the point of Dead-Man, we saw the wickiups of the Paiutes and the little hearth-fires all awink among the sage. They had a look of home.

"There's some," said the driver to the desert at large, "that thinks Indians ain't properly folks, but just a kind of cattle." Then, as we jolted forward in a chuck, he swore deeply and brought the team about, putting back my instinctive motion to steady the lurching stage with a gesture so sharp and repellant that I sat up suddenly in offence.

"Don't you go for to mind me," he said, only half mindful himself of what he had done, and went on staring after the hearth-fires of the Paiutes. By which I knew there was a story there that had something to do with the twilight fires and the homey look of the little huts. Hours later, when we came out on the mesa above Red Rock, white star-froth flecking the black vault over us, and the road white between the miles of low black sage before, we had got to this point in it.

"It was out there," he said, waving his whip toward the gulf of blackness, "when I was doin' assessment work for McKenna, nigh to the end of nowhere, I...took up with an Indian woman." He hurried past this admission with intent to cover it from possible reproach, telling how McKenna had dumped him with three months' grub by a water-hole called Agua Dulce, distant a mile or two from the claims he was expected to work.

"Because," he said, "it was cheaper than packin' water, me bein' alone, and McKenna, for some reason, I never rightly guessed, keen to keep the business on the quiet. McKenna would be visitin' me once a month or so, and I 'lowed I wouldn't lonesome much," he laughed, "and I didn't after I...took up with Catameneda.

"Seems like white women can't get to understand why a man takes up with a *mahala*. They think it's just badness, and so they're down on it...Maybe it is with some...but not when they are like...like me...and Catameneda...There's something away down in a man that his own women folks never understand...an' you spend all your life trying to keep them from understanding...though when there's one that does she plays hell with you...It ain't badness...I don't know rightly what, only it ain't all bad...but Catameneda...she understood...and I was glad to have her."

The wind died along the sage, and there was no sound under heaven louder than the gride of the wheels and the clink of the harness, chains. Presently he returned upon his track to say that he had been a month at Agua Dulce, going and returning from the mines each day to his little camp kit, laid under a square of canvas with stones upon it to keep it from the wind. He had cached the bulk of his supplies behind the spring, and congratulated himself on it when at the close of one day he found a camp of Indians at Agua Dulce.

"You know how it is with these desert tribes," said the stage-driver: "every camp looks as if it might have been there for a hundred years, and when they go there's no more left than a last year's bird-nest. They just scramble up out of nothing and melt away in the sand like a horned toad. But they was friendly...sort of...when you got to know them...and the men talked English considerable....Evenings when a kind of creepy chill comes on, they get around their little fires and crack their jokes...good jokes, too...there was one old buck real comical,...he used to explain them in English afterward. And when they sang their songs...when the fires were lit and the voices came out of the dark, and you couldn't see the dirt nor the color of their skins, you would sort of forget they wasn't your own folks.

"And so," he said, after a longer silence, "when the camp went on another *pasear*...Catameneda...she stayed." That was all I was ever to know of that phase of it. "Catameneda stayed." That and the flicker in his voice cast up from the things in him that only the Indian woman could understand, that lit the situation through his scanty speech like the glow of those vanished fires.

"It was a sort of pretty place at Agua Dulce," said he. "The spring came out from the black rock into a basin with a gurgly sound. There was a pink flowering bush behind it, and a smitch of green where it ran over into the sand...and the rest was sage-bush, little and low; and crumply, colored hills. There were doves came and built in the flowering shrubs, for they hadn't no fear of man...and 'Maneda, she fed them."

He was silent, letting his whip-lash trail outside in the sand, and I had a long time in which to consider how young he was, and how much younger he must have been when he drank sweet water out there at Agua Dulce, before he began again.

"She was mighty lovin'," he said; and suddenly I saw the whole tale as I had constructed it ahead of his halting speech fall apart, and rebuild itself to a larger plan as he went on to say how, when he came from the mine at night and had no caress for her, she would begin to droop and to grieve, to flood with tears and heavy sobbing like a hurt child, which he could still in a moment with a hand upon her hair; and how he would pretend a harshness at times to see her flash and glow with the assurance of tenderness renewed, which he laughed at her for never learning. Sweet water, indeed, at Agua Dulce!

By this I knew the story had come to some uncommon end that lifted it beyond the vulgar adventure of satiety and desertion, for there was no yellowness in the boy that he should blab upon the tenderness of women. There was a good hour yet until we came to Coyote Holes, and I meant to have it all out of him by then. The end had come very quickly. It began in their growing careless through happiness and neglecting the cache. Then one day, when he was at the mine, and Catameneda setting snares for quail in the black rock, a thieving prospector rifled it and left them wofully short of food. Five days of desertness lay between them and any possible base of supplies, and McKenna was not due until the twenty-ninth. They took stock and decided to hold out on short rations until he came. They were very merry about it, being so young, and Catameneda knew the way to piece out their fare with roots and herbs. She promised him he should learn to eat lizards yet, as Indians do. And then suddenly the boy fell sick of a dysentery which he thought might have come from some mistaken economy of Catameneda's in the matter of canned food; and while he was prostrated with that came the sand-storm. The girl had sensed it, Indian fashion, days before it came, but he was loggy with weakness and the want of proper care, and let her warning pass. Then came a night of gusty flaws; the morning showed a wall of yellow cloud advancing from the south.

All that country around Agua Dulce is solid rock and fluctuant sand that moves before the wind with a small, shrill rustle, and no trail can lie in it when the wind blows more than twenty-four hours. On this occasion it blew for three days.

"Time was," said the driver, "I'd lie awake nights to mill it over and over. Times I'd think I could have done better, times again I didn't know as I could. I was too sick to think much, and 'Maneda was mighty uneasy, all for getting' forward on the trail to meet McKenna, who would be comin' toward us. She calculated he would stop at Beeman's till the storm was past, not knowin' we were short. And the wind would blow three days. I don't know how she knew, but she knew. She kept holding up her fingers to show me how many days, and forgetting what English I had taught her; and between that and me being fair locoed with sickness, I gave in. I don't know if we wouldn't have done better to stick it out at Agua Dulce. And, again, I don't know as we would."

They took the canteen and such food as they had and set out for the next water-hole; by noon the sand storm overtook them. The push of the wind was steady, and they tacked along the edge of it without too much discomfort. The boy was pitifully weak, and Catameneda laughed as she braced him with her firm, young body. The dark fell early, the wind increased and roared against them; the boy, chilled in the night, grew feverish, and Catameneda was reduced to hiding the canteen to save their scanty drink. By all counts they should have reached the first water-hole that day, but did not until the next noon. And the storm had been before them. The sand lay clean white and drifted smooth over all that place. Come another winter, the spring would work its way to the surface perhaps, but now they could not so much as guess where to dig for it. They walked on and on, Catameneda leading with his hand in hers. This day they faced the wind. The girl's hair blew back, and he held it to his eyes to shield them from the tormenting sting of the sand. The water and food held out better than he expected.

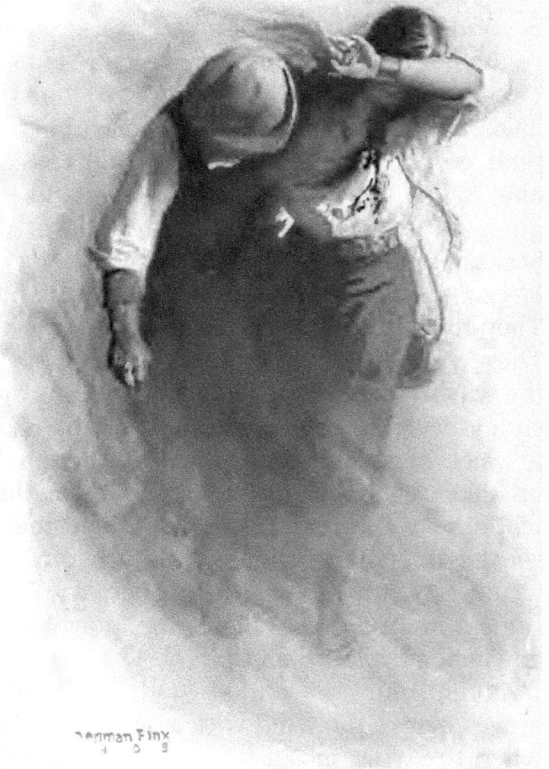

Catameneda Laughed As She Braced Him with Her Firm Young Body

He said that he thought Catameneda must have waked him in the night, when there was a lull in the wind, for he seemed to remember crawling long distances on hands and knees, and other times he leaned upon her body and heard her voice, but did not seem to see her. Always they travelled in a fury of wind and a biting smother of sand.

"I don't know how 'Maneda pulled me through," he said, "but she did. All I remember was the beginning of the basalt wall at the root of Black Mountain, and right away after that the drip of the spring, though it's two mile from where the rock begins. I was long past bein' hungry, but I jest naturally wallowed in that water, and it ain't any great water neither, not like the water at Agua Dulce. But Catameneda she didn't seem to care for none."

42

He paused so long here that if I had not known his kind very well, I should have thought it all the story he meant to let me have; but at last:

"I reckon I was light-headed," he said, "else I should have sensed what was the matter; but I don't know but it was best as it was. I couldn't have done nothin'. We lay on the sand far spent and sick, the wind was going down, and we could breathe better under the wall. I heard her kind of choke up every little, and by-and-by she was talking quiet like, in her own language, and I made out she wanted her mother...she wasn't more than seventeen, I should think...It was cold, too, and I'd lost my blanket somewhere back on the trail, not bein' able to say where...I snuggled her up in my arms, kind of shivery like...and by-and-by...she knew me, puttin' her hand up to my face, a way she had...and sayin' in English, as I had taught her, 'Vera good boy, mucha like.' And it didn't seem no time at all after that when it was broad morning and the wind was down...her hair on my face...and she was heavy on my arm.

"I sat up and laid her on the sand...It was too much for her...all she had been through...bein' so young...and she had given me all the food and all the water...though I hadn't felt to know it before. I knew it as soon as I looked at her...I reckon she had a hemorrhage or something...there was blood on her face and sleeves like she wiped it from her mouth."

Out in the blackness toward Agua Dulce a coyote howled and night freshened for a sign of morning.

"McKenna came through by noon, and we buried her," he finished, simply, "under a pink flowering bush, because she loved it. I worked on a ranch in the valley for two years after that...I couldn't seem to abide the desert for a spell...nor the little fires...but I got over that...you know how that is."

"Yes, I know how that is."

"But I don't suppose anybody knows," he went on, reflectively, "how it is that I don't think of her dead any more, nor any of that hard time we had...only sometimes when it's spring like this, and I smell sage-brush burning...it reminds me...of some loving way she had out there...at Agua Dulce."

A man's story like that is always so much more satisfactory because he tells you all the story there is, what happened to him, and how he felt about it, supposing his feelings are any part of the facts in the case; but with a woman it is not so. She never knows much about her feelings, unless they are pertinent to the story, and then she leaves them out.

Chapter Eight - The Woman at the Eighteen-Mile

I HAD long wished to write a story of Death Valley that should be its final word. It was to be so chosen from the limited sort of incidents that could occur there, so charged with the still ferocity of its moods that I should at length be quit of its obsession, free to concern myself about other affairs. And from the moment of hearing of the finding of Lang's body at Dead Man's Spring I knew I had struck upon the trail of that story.

It was a teamster who told it, stopping over the night at McGee's, a big, slow man, face and features all of a bluntness, as if he had been dropped before the clay was set. He had a big, blunt voice through which his words rolled, dulled along the edges. The same accident that had flattened the outlines of his nose and chin must have happened to his mind, for he was never able to deliver more than the middle of an idea, without any definiteness as to where it began or ended and what it stood next to. He called the dead man Long, and failed to remember who was supposed to have killed him, and what about.

We had fallen a-talking round the fire of Convict Lake, and the teamster had handed up the incident of Dead Man's Spring as the only thing in his experience that matched with the rooted horror of its name. He had been of the party that recovered the body, and what had stayed with him was the sheer torment of the journey across Death Valley, the aching heat, the steady, sickening glare, the uncertainty as to whether there was a body in the obliterated grave, whether it was Lang's body, and whether they would be able to prove it; and then the exhuming of the dead, like the one real incident in a fever dream. He was very sure of the body, done up in an Indian blanket striped red and black, with a rope around it like a handle, convenient for carrying. But he had forgotten what set the incident in motion, or what became of Lang after that, if it really were Lang in the blanket.

Then I heard of the story again between Red Rock and Coyote Holes, about moon-set, when the stage labored up the long gorge, waking to hear the voices of the passengers run on steadily with the girding of the sand and the rattle of harness-chains, run on and break and eddy around Dead Man's Springs, and back up in turgid pools of comment and speculation, falling in shallows of miner's talk, lost at last in a waste of ledges and contracts and forgotten strikes. Waking and falling asleep again, the story shaped itself of the largeness of the night; and then the two men got down at Coyote Holes an hour before dawn, and I knew no more of them, neither face nor name. But what I had heard of the story confirmed it exactly, the story I had so long sought.

Those who have not lived in a mining country cannot understand how it is possible for whole communities to be so disrupted by the failure of a lode or a fall in the price of silver, that I could live seven years within a day's journey of Dead Man's Spring and not come upon anybody who could give me the whole of that story. I went about asking for it, and got sticks and straws. There was a man who had kept bar in Tio Juan at the time, and had been the first to notice Whitmark's dealing with the Shoshone who was supposed to have stolen the body after it was dug up. There was a Mexican who had been the last to see Lang alive and might have told somewhat, but death got him before I did. Once, at a great dinner in San Francisco, a large, positive man with a square forehead and a face below it that somehow implied he had shaped it so butting his way through life, across the table two places down, caught at some word of mine, leaning forward above the bank of carnations that divided the cloth.

"Queer thing happened up in that country to a friend of mine, Whitmark -". But the toast-master cut *him* off. All this time the story glimmered like a summer island in a mist, through every man's talk about it, grew and allured, caressing the soul. It had warmth and amplitude, like a thing palpable to be stroked. There was a mine in it, a murder and a mystery, great sacrifice, Shoshones, dark and incredibly discreet, and the magnetic will of a man making manifest through all these; there were lonely water-holes, deserted camps where coyotes hunted in the streets, fatigues and dreams and voices of the night. And at the last it appeared there was a woman in it.

Curiously, long before I learned of her connection with the story, I had known and liked her for a certain effect she had of being warmed and nourished from within. There was about her a spark, a nuance that men mistook never more than once, as the stage-driver told me confidently a vitality that had nothing, absolutely nothing, but the blank occasionless life of the desert to sustain it. She was one of the very few people I had known able to keep a soul alive and glowing in the wilderness, and I was to find out that she kept it so against the heart of my story. Mine! I called it so by that time; but hers was the right, though she had no more pertinence to the plot than most women have to desert affairs.

She was the Woman of the Eighteen-Mile House. She had the desert mark upon her - lean figure, wasted bosom, the sharp, upright furrow between the eyes, the burned, tawny skin, with the pallid streak of the dropped eyelids, and of course I suppose she knew her husband from among the lean, sidling, vacuous-looking Borderers; but I couldn't have identified him, so like he was to the other feckless men whom the desert sucks dry and keeps dangling like gourds on a string. Twenty-five years they had drifted from up Bodie way, around Panimint, toward Mojave, worse housed and fed than they might have been in the ploughed lands, and without having hit upon the fortune which is primarily the object of every desert adventure. And when people have been as long as that among the Lost Borders there is not the slightest possibility of their coming to anything else. And still the Woman's soul was palpitant and enkindled. At the last, Mayer - that was the husband's name - had settled at the Eighteen-Mile House to care for the stage relays, and I had met the Woman, halting there with the stage or camping nights on some slower passage.

At the time I learned of her connection with the Whitmark affair, the story still wanted some items of motive and understanding, a knowledge of the man himself, some account of his three months' *pasear* into the hills beyond Mesquite, which certainly had to do with the affair of the mine, but of which he would never be persuaded to speak. And I made perfectly sure of getting the rest of it from the Woman at the Eighteen-Mile.

It was full nine o'clock before the Woman's household was all settled and she had come out upon the stoop of the Eighteen-Mile House to talk, the moon coming up out of Shoshone land, all the hollow of the desert falling away before us, filled with the glitter of that surpassing wonder, the moon-mirage. Never mind what went before to draw her to the point of talking; it could have come about as simply as my saying, "I mean to print this story as I find it," and she would have had to talk to save it. Consider how still it was. Off to the right the figures of my men under their blankets stretched along the ground. Not a leaf to rustle, not a bough to creak. No grass to whisper in the wind, only stiff, scant shrubs and the sandy hills like shoals at the bottom of a lake of light. I could see the Woman's profile, thin and fine against the moon, and when she put up her hand to drag down the thick, careless coil of her hair, I guessed we were close upon the heart of the story. And for her the heart of the story was the man, Whitmark.

She had been, at the time he came into the country seventeen years before, that which the world knows so little what to do with that it mostly throws away - a good woman with great power and possibilities of passion. Whitmark stood for the best she had known, I should have said from all I learned, just a clean-minded, acute, tolerably cultivated American business man with an obsession for accomplishing results.

He had been sent out to look after a mine to which the title was not clear, and there were counter machinations to take it away from him. This much may be told without breach, for, as it turned out, I was not to write that story, after all; at least, not in the lifetime of the Woman at the Eighteen-Mile. And the crux of the story to her was one little, so little, moment, that owing to Whitmark's having been taken with pneumonia within a week afterward, was rendered fixed beyond change or tarnish of time.

When all this was going forward the Mayers kept a miner's boarding-house at Tio Juan, where Whitmark was in and out; and the Woman, who from the first had been attracted by the certain stamp of competency and power, began to help him with warnings, intimations of character and local prejudice, afterward with information which got him the reputation of almost supernatural penetration.

There were reasons why, during his darkest time, Whitmark could find nobody but the Indians and the Woman to trust. Well, he had been wise enough to trust her, and it was plain to see from her account of it that this was the one occasion in life when her soul had stretched itself, observed, judged, wrought, and felt to the full of its power.

She loved him; yes, perhaps - I do not know - if you call love that soul service of a good woman to a man she may not touch. Whitmark had chil-dren back East, and a wife whom he had married for all the traditions of niceness and denial and abnegation which men demand of the women they expect to marry, and find savorless so often when they are married to it. He had never known what it meant to have a woman concerned in his work, running neck and neck with it, divining his need, supplementing it not with the merely feminine trick of making him more complacent with himself, but with vital remedies and aids. And once he had struck the note of the West, he kindled to the event and enlarged his spirit. The two must have had great moments at the heart of that tremendous coil of cir-cumstance. All this the Woman conveyed to me by the simplest telling of the story as it happened: "I said...and he did...the Indian went..."

I sat within the shallow shadow of the eaves experiencing the full-throated satisfaction of old prospectors over the feel of pay dirt, rubbing it between the thumb and palm, swearing over it softly below the breath. It was as good as that. And I was never to have it! For one thing the Wom-an made plain to me in the telling was the guilt of Whitmark. Though there was no evidence by which the court could hold him, though she did not believe it, though the fulness of her conviction intrigued me into be-lieving that it did not matter so much what he was - the only way to write that story successfully was to fix forever against Whitmark's name its damning circumstance. The affair had been a good deal noised about at the time, and through whatever illusion of altered name and detail, was bound to be recognized and made much of in the newspapers. The Wom-an of the Eighteen-Mile saw that. Suddenly she broke off the telling to show me her poor heart, shrivelling as I knew hearts to warp and shrink in the aching wilderness, this one occasion rendering it serviceable like a hearth-fire in an empty room.

"It was a night like this he went away," said the Woman, stirring to point to the solemn moonlight poured over all the world.

That was after twenty-two months of struggle had left Whitmark in possession of the property. He was on his way then to visit his family, whom he had seen but once in that time, and was to come again to put in operation the mine he had so hardly won. It was, it should have been, an hour ripe with satisfaction.

"He was to take the stage which passed through Bitter Wells at ten that night," said she, "and I rode out with him he had asked me from Tio Juan, to bring back the horses. We started at sunset and reached the Wells a quarter of an hour before the time.

"The moon was half high when the sun went down, and I was very happy, because it had all come out so well, and he was to come again in two months. We talked as we rode. I told you he was a cheerful man. All the time when it looked as if he might be tried for his life, the worse it looked the more his spirits rose. He would have laughed if he had heard he was to be hung. But

The Moon was Half High When the Sun Went Down

that night there was a trouble upon him. It grew as we rode. His face drew, his breath came sighing. He seemed always on the point of speaking and did not. It was as if he had something to say that must be said, and at the moment of opening his lips it escaped him. In the moonlight I saw his mouth working, and nothing came from it. If I spoke the trouble went out of his face, and when I left off it came again, puzzled wonder and pain. I know now!" said the Woman, shaking forward her thick hair, "that it was a warning, a presentiment. I have heard of such things, and it seems as if I should have felt it too, hovering in the air like that. But I was glad because it had all come out so well and I had had a hand in it. Besides, it was not for me." She turned toward me then for the first time, her hair falling forward to encompass all her face but the eyes, wistful with the desire to have me understand how fine this man was in every worldly point, how far above her, and how honored she was to have been the witness of the intimation of his destiny. I said quickly the thing that was expected of me, which was not the thing I thought, and gave her courage for going on.

"Yet," she said, "I was not entirely out of it, because the thing he said at the last, *when* he said it, did not seem the least strange to me, though afterward, of course, when I thought of it, it was the strangest goodbye I had ever heard.

"We had got down and stood between the horses, and the stage was coming in. We heard the sand fret under it, and the moonlight was a cold weight laid upon the world. He took my hand and held it against his breast so - and said - Oh, I am perfectly sure of the words; he said, 'I have *missed* you so.' Just that, not good-bye, and not *shall* miss you, but 'I *have* missed you *so.*'

"Like that," she said, her hands still clasped above her wasted bosom, the quick spirit glowing through it like wine in a turgid glass - "like that," she said. But, no; whatever the phrase implied of the failure of the utterly safe and respectable life to satisfy the inmost hunger of the man, it could never have had in it the pain of her impassioned, lonely years. If it had been the one essential word the Desert strives to say it would have been pronounced like that.

"And it was not until the next day," she went on, "it occurred to me that was a strange thing to say to a woman he had seen two or three times a week for nearly two years. But somehow it seemed to me clearer when I heard a week later that he was dead. He had taken cold on the way home, and died after three days. His wife wrote me; it was a very nice letter; she said he told her I had been kind to him. Kind!" She broke off, and far out under the moon rose the thin howl of coyotes running together in the pack. "And that," said the Woman, "is why I made you promise at the beginning that if I told you all I knew about Whitmark and Lang you would not use it."

I jumped. She had done that, and I had promised light-heartedly. People nearly always exact that sort of an assurance in the beginning of confidences, like a woman wanting to be told she is of nobler courage at the moment of committing an indiscretion, a concession to the sacredness of personal experience which always seems so much less once it is delivered, they can be persuaded to forego the promise of inviolateness. I always promise and afterward persuade. But not the Woman of the Eighteen-Mile. If Whitmark had lived he would have come back and proved his worth, cleared himself by his life and works. As it stood, by the facts against him, he was most utterly given over to ill-repute. The singularity of the incident, the impossibility of its occurring in any place but Death Valley, conspired to fix the ineffaceable stain upon his wife and his children, for, by the story as I should write it, he ought to have been hung. No use to say modestly that the scratchings of my pen would never reach them. If it were not the biggest story of the desert ever written, I had no wish to write it. And there was the Woman. The story was all she had, absolutely all of heart-stretching, of enlargement and sustenance. What she thought about it was that that last lusive moment when she touched the forecast shadow of his destiny was to bind her to save his credit for his children's sake. One must needs be faithful to one's experiences when there are so few of them.

She said something like that, gathering up her hair in both hands, standing before me in the wan revealing light. The mark of the desert was on her. Heart of desolation! But I knew what pinchings of the spirit went to make that mark!

"It was a promise," she said.

"It is a promise."

But I caught myself in the reservation that it should not mean beyond the term of her life.

Every now and then arises some city-surfeited demand for a great primitive love-story: it is usually a Professor in the English Department or some young man on the Daily News at fifteen per who dreams of writing it. Only those who have learned it at firsthand understand that there is no such thing; that primitive love is the most complaisant, that is to say, the most serviceable to Life of all human passions.

But when we magnify it with bonds it chafes itself to dramatic proportions. Love is Life's own way of reducing the clash of human contacts in order that the pair may turn a more opposing front to the adversary, the Wilderness.

It springs up, oh, it springs up, as Life divinely meant it, wherever, in the press of existence, men and women come together; requires, when the conditions are of a simpleness called primitive, no other inducement. But Life did not invent Society, seems somehow never to be properly aware of it; though it justifies itself of Love, cannot yet square with Respectability, with the Church and Property. Threading through these, Love weaves the fascinating intricacy of story, but here in the Borders, where the warp runs loose and wide, the pattern has not that richness it should show in the close fabric of civilization. If it lived next door to you, you probably, wouldn't have anything to do with it.

50

Chapter Nine - The Fakir

WHENEVER I come up to judgment, and am hard pushed to make good on my own account (as I expect to be), I shall mention the case of Netta Saybrick, for on the face of it, and by all the traditions in which I was bred, I behaved rather handsomely. I say on the face of it, for except in the matter of keeping my mouth shut afterward, I am not so sure I had anything to do with the affair. It was one of those incidents that from some crest of sheer inexplicableness seems about to direct the imagination over vast tracts of human experience, only to fall away into a pit of its own digging, all fouled with weed and sand. But, by keeping memory and attention fixed on its pellucid instant as it mounted against the sun, I can still see the Figure shining through it as I saw it that day at Posada, with the glimmering rails of the P. and S. running out behind it, thin lines of light toward the bar of Heaven.

Up till that time Netta Saybrick had never liked me, though I never laid it to any other account than Netta's being naturally a little fool; afterward she explained to me that it was because she thought I gave myself airs. The Saybricks lived in the third house from mine, around the corner, so that our back doors overlooked each other, and up till the coming of Doctor Challoner there had never been anything in Netta's conduct that the most censorious of the villagers could remark upon. Nor afterward, for that matter. The Saybricks had been married four years, and the baby was about two. He was not an interesting child to anybody but his mother, and even Netta was sometimes thought to be not quite absorbed in him.

Saybrick was a miner, one of the best drillers in our district, and consequently away from home much of the time. Their house was rather larger than their needs, and Netta, to avoid loneliness more than for profit, let out a room or two. That was the way she happened to fall into the hands of the Fakir.

Franklin Challoner had begun by being a brilliant and promising student of medicine. I had known him when his natural gifts prophesied the unusual, but I had known him rather better than most, and I was not surprised to have him turn up five years later at Maverick as a Fakir.

It had begun in his being poor, and having to work his way through the Medical College at the cost of endless pains and mortification to himself. Like most brilliant people, Challoner was sensitive and had an enormous egotism, and, what nearly always goes with it, the faculty of being horribly fascinating to women. It was thought very creditable of him to have put himself through college at his own charge, though in reality it proved a great social waste. I have a notion that the courage, endurance, and steadfastness which should have done Frank Challoner a lifetime was squeezed out of him by the stress of those overworked, starved, mortifying years. His egotism made it important to his happiness to keep the centre of any stage, and this he could do in school by sheer brilliance of scholarship and the distinction of his struggles. But afterward, when he had to establish himself without capital among strangers, he found himself impoverished of manliness. Always there was the compelling need of his temperament to stand well with people, and almost the only means of accomplishing it his poverty allowed was the dreadful facility with which he made himself master of women. I suppose this got his real ability discredited among his professional fellows. Between that and the sharp need of money, and the incredible appetite which people have for being fooled, somewhere in the Plateau of Fatigue between promise and accomplishment, Frank Challoner lost himself. Therefore, I was not surprised when he turned up finally at Maverick, lecturing on phrenology, and from the shape of their craniums advising country people of their proper careers at three dollars a sitting. He advertised to do various things in the way of medical practice that had a dubious sound.

It was court week when he came, and the only possible lodging to be found at Netta Saybrick's. Doctor Challoner took the two front rooms as being best suited to his clients and himself, and I believe he did very well. I was not particularly pleased to see him, on account of having known him before, not wishing to prosecute the acquaintance; and about that time Indian George brought me word that a variety of *redivivus* long sought was blooming that year on a certain clayey tract over toward Waban. It was not supposed to flower oftener than once in seven years, and I was five days finding it. That was why I never knew what went on at Mrs. Saybrick's. Nobody else did, apparently, for I never heard a breath of gossip, and *that* must have been Doctor Challoner's concern, for I am sure Netta would never have known how to avoid it.

Netta was pretty, and Saybrick had been gone five months. Challoner had a thin, romantic face, and eyes - even I had to admit the compelling attraction of his eyes; and his hands were fine and white. Saybrick's hands were cracked, broken-nailed, a driller's hands, and one of them was twisted from the time he was leaded, working on the Lucky Jim. If it came to that, though, Netta's husband might have been anything he pleased, and Challoner would still have had his way with her. He always did with women, as if to make up for not having it with the world. And the life at Maverick was deadly, appallingly dull. The stark houses, the rubbishy streets, the women who went about in them in calico wrappers, the draggling speech of the men, the wide, shadowless table-lands, the hard, bright skies, and the days all of one pattern, that went so stilly by that you only knew it was afternoon when you smelled the fried cabbage Mrs. Mulligan was cooking for supper.

At this distance I cannot say that I blamed Netta, am not sure of not being glad that she had her hour of the rose-red glow - *if* she had it. You are to bear in mind that all this time I was camping out in the creosote belt on the slope of Waban, and as to what had really happened neither Netta nor Challoner ever said a word. I keep saying things like this about Netta's being pretty and all, just as if I thought they had anything to do with it; truth is, the man had just a gift of taking souls, and I, even I, judicious and disapproving - but you shall hear.

At that time the stage from Maverick was a local affair going down to Posada, where passengers from the P. and S. booked for the Mojave line, returning after a wait of hours on the same day.

It happened that the morning I came back from Waban, Doctor Challoner left Maverick.

Being saddle weary, I had planned to send on the horses by Indian George, and take the stage where it crossed my trail an hour out from Posada, going home on it in the afternoon. I remember poking the botany - case under the front seat and turning round to be hit straight between the eyes, as it were, by Netta Say brick and Doctor Challoner. The doctor was wearing his usual air of romantic mystery; wearing it a little awry - or perhaps it was only knowing the man that made me read the perturbation under it. But it was plain to see what Netta was about. Her hat was tilted by the jolting of the stage, white alkali dust lay heavy on the folds of her dress, and she never *would* wear hair-pins enough; but there was that in every turn and posture, in every note of her flat, childish voice, that acknowledged the man beside her. Her excitement was almost febrile. It was part of Netta's unsophistication that she seemed not to know that she gave herself away, and the witness of it was that she had brought the baby.

You would not have believed that any woman would plan to run away with a man like Frank Challoner and take that great, heavy-headed, drooling child. But that is what Netta had done. I am not sure it was maternal instinct, either; she probably did not know what else to do with him. He had pale, protruding eyes and reddish hair, and every time he clawed at the doctor's sleeve I could see the man withhold a shudder.

I suppose it was my being in a manner confounded by this extraordinary situation that made it possible for Doctor Challoner to renew his acquaintance with more warmth than the facts allowed. He fairly pitched himself into an intimacy of reminiscence, and it was partly to pay him for this, I suppose, and partly to gratify a natural curiosity, that made me so abrupt with him afterward. I remember looking around, when we got down, at the little station where I must wait two hours for the return stage, at the seven unpainted pine cabins, at the eating-house, and the store, and the two saloons, in the instant hope of refuge, and then out across the alkali flat fringed with sparse, unwholesome pickle-weed, and deciding that that would not do, and then turning round to take the situation by the throat, as it were. There was Netta, with that great child dragging on her arm and her hat still on one side, with a silly consciousness of Doctor Challoner's movements, and he still trying for the jovial note of old acquaintances met by chance. In a moment more I had him around the corner of the station-house and out with my question.

"Doctor Challoner, are you running away with Netta Saybrick?"

"Well, no," trying to carry it jauntily; "I think she is running away with me." Then, all his pretension suddenly sagging on him like an empty cayaque: "On my soul, I don't know what's got into the woman. I was as surprised as you were when she got on the stage with me" - on my continuing to look steadily at him - "she was a pretty little thing...and the life is devilish dull there...I suppose I flirted a little" - blowing himself out, as it were, with an assumption of honesty - "on my word, there was nothing more than that."

Flirted! He called it that; but women do not take their babies and run away from home for the sake of a little flirting. The life was devilish dull - did he need to tell me that! And she was pretty - well, whatever had happened he was bound to tell me that it was nothing, and I was bound to behave as if I believed him.

"She will go back," he began to say, looking bleak and drawn in the searching light. "She must go back! She must!"

"Well, maybe you can persuade her," said I; but I relented after that enough to take care of the baby while he and Netta went for a walk.

The whole mesa and the flat crawled with heat, and the steel rails ran on either side of them like thin fires, as if the slagged track were the appointed way that Netta had chosen to walk. They went out as far as the section-house and back toward the deserted station till I could almost read their faces clear, and turned again, back and forth through the heat-fogged atmosphere like the figures in a dream. I could see this much from their postures, that Challoner was trying to hold to some consistent attitude which he had adopted, and Netta wasn't understanding it. I could see her throw out her hands in a gesture of abandonment, and then I saw her stand as if the Pit yawned under her feet. The baby slept on a station bench, and I kept the flies from him with a branch of pickle-weed. I was out of it, smitten anew with the utter inutility of all the standards which

54

were not bred of experience, but merely came down to me with the family teaspoons. Seen by the fierce desert light they looked like the spoons, thin and worn at the edges. I should have been ashamed to offer them to Netta Saybrick. It was this sense of detached helplessness toward the life at Maverick that Netta afterward explained she and the other women sensed but misread in me. They couldn't account for it on any grounds except that I felt myself above them. And all the time I was sick with the strained, meticulous inadequacy of my own soul. I understood well enough, then, that the sense of personal virtue comes to most women through an intervening medium of sedulous social guardianship. It is only when they love that it reaches directly to the centre of consciousness, as if it were ultimately nothing more than the instinctive movement of right love to preserve itself by a voluntary seclusion. It was not her faithlessness to Saybrick that tormented Netta out there between the burning rails; it was going back to him that was the intolerable offence. Passion had come upon her like a flame-burst, heaven-sent; she justified it on the grounds of its completeness, and lacked the sophistication for any other interpretation.

Challoner was a bad man, but he was not bad enough to reveal to Netta Saybrick the vulgar cheapness of his own relation to the incident. Besides, he hadn't time. In two hours the return stage for Maverick left the station, and he could never in that time get Netta Saybrick to realize the gulf between his situation and hers.

He came back to the station after a while on some pretext, and said, with his back to Netta, moving his lips with hardly any sound: "She must go back on the stage. She must!" Then with a sudden setting of his jaws, "You've got to help me." He sat down beside me, and began to devote himself to the baby and the flies.

Netta stood out for a while expecting him, and then came and sat provisionally on the edge of the station platform, ready at the slightest hint of an opportunity to carry him away into the glimmering heat out toward the stationhouse, and resume the supremacy of her poor charms.

She was resenting my presence as an interference, and I believe always cherished a thought that but for the accident of my being there the incident might have turned out differently. I could see that Challoner's attitude, whatever it was, was beginning to make itself felt. She was looking years older, and yet somehow pitifully puzzled and young, as if the self of her had had a wound which her intelligence had failed to grasp. I could see, too, that Challoner had made up his mind to be quit of her, quietly if he could, but at any risk of a scene, still to be quit. And it was forty minutes till stage-time.

Challoner sat on the bare station bench with his arm out above the baby protectingly - it was a manner always effective - and began to talk about "goodness," of all things in the world. Don't ask me what he said. It was the sort of talk many women would have called beautiful, and though it was mostly addressed to me, it was every word of it directed to Netta Saybrick's soul. Much of it went high and wide, but I could catch -the pale reflection of it in her face like a miner guessing the sort of day it is from the glimmer of it on a puddle at the bottom of a shaft. In it Netta saw a pair of heroic figures renouncing a treasure they had found for the sake of the bitter goodness by which the world is saved. They had had the courage to take it while they could, but were much too exemplary to enjoy it at the cost of pain to any other heart. He started with the assumption that she meant to go back to Maverick, and recurred to it with a skilful and hypnotic insistence, painting upon her mind by large and general inference the picture of himself, helped greatly in his career by her noble renunciation of him. As a matter of fact, Saybrick, if his wife really had gone away with Doctor Challoner, would have followed him up and shot him, I suppose, and no end of vulgar and disagreeable things might have come from the affair; but Challoner managed to keep it on so high a plane that even I never thought of them until long afterward. And right here is where the uncertainty as to the part I really played begins. I can never make up my mind whether Challoner, from long practice in such affairs, had hit upon just the right note of extrication, or whether, cornered, he fell back desperately on the eternal Tightness. And what was he, to know lightness at his need?

He was terribly in earnest, holding Netta's eyes with his own; his forehead sweated, hollows showed about his eyes, and the dreadful slackness of the corner of the mouth that comes of the whole mind being drawn away upon the object of attack to the neglect of its defences. He was so bent on getting Netta fixed in the idea that she must go back to Maverick that if she had not been a good deal of a fool she must have seen that he had given away the whole situation into my hands. I believed - I hope - I did the right thing, but I am not sure I could have helped taking the cue which was pressed upon me; he was as bad as they made them, but there I was lending my whole soul to the accomplishment of his purpose, which was, briefly, to get comfortably off from an occasion in which he had behaved very badly.

All this time Challoner kept a conscious attention on the stage stables far at the other end of the shadeless street. The moment he saw the driver come out of it with the horses, the man's soul fairly creaked with the release of tension. It released, too, an accession of that power of personal fascination for which he was remarkable.

Netta sat with her back to the street, and the beautiful solicitude with which he took up the baby at that moment, smoothed its dress and tied on its little cap, had no significance for her. It was not until she heard the rattle of the stage turning into the road that she stood up suddenly, alarmed. Challoner put the baby into my arms.

Did I tell you that all this time between me and this man there ran the inexplicable sense of being bonded together; the same suggestion of a superior and exclusive intimacy which ensnared poor Netta Say brick no doubt, the absolute call of self and sex by which a man, past all reasonableness and belief, ranges a woman on his side. He was a Fakir, a common quack, a scoundrel if you will, but there was the call. I had answered it. I was under the impression, though not remembering what he said, when he had handed me that great lump of a child, that I had received a command to hold on to it, to get into the stage with it, and not to give it up on any consideration; and without saying anything, I had promised.

I do not know if it was the look that must have passed between us at that, or the squeal of the running-gear that shattered her dream, but I perceived on the instant that Netta had had a glimpse of where she stood. She saw herself for the moment a fallen woman, forsaken, despised. There was the Pit before her which Challoner's desertion and my knowledge of it had digged. She clutched once at her bosom and at her skirts as if already she heard the hiss of crawling shame. Then it was that Challoner turned toward her with the Look.

It rose in his face and streamed to her from his eyes as though it were the one thing in the world of a completeness equal to the anguish in her breast, as though, before it rested there, it had been through all the troubled intricacies of sin, and come upon the root of a superior fineness that every soul feels piteously to lie at the back of all its own affronting vagaries, brooding over it in a large, gentle way. It was the forgiveness - nay, the obliteration of offence - and the most Challoner could have known of forgiveness was his own great need of it. Out of that Look I could see the woman's soul rising rehabilitated, astonished, and on the instant, out there beyond the man and the woman, between the thin fiery lines of the rails, leading back to the horizon, the tall, robed Figure writing in the sand.

Oh, it was a hallucination, if you like, of the hour, the place, the perturbed mind, the dazzling glimmer of the alkali flat, of the incident of a sinful woman and a common fakir, faking an absolution that he might the more easily avoid an inconvenience, and I the tool made to see incredibly by some trick of suggestion how impossible it should be that any but the chief of sinners should understand forgiveness. But the Look continued to hold the moment in sojution, while the woman climbed out of the Pit. I

57

saw her put out her hand with the instinctive gesture of the sinking, and Challoner take it with the formality of farewell; and as the dust of the arriving stage billowed up between them, the Figure turned, fading, dissolving...but with the Look, consoling, obliterating...He too...!

"It was very good of you, Mrs. Saybrick, to give me so much of a good-bye..." Challoner was saying as he put Netta into the stage; and then to me, "You must take good care of her ...good-bye."

"Good-bye, Frank" - I had never called Doctor Challoner by his name before. I did not like him well enough to call him by it at any time, but there was the Look; it had reached out and enwrapped me in a kind of rarefied intimacy of extenuation and understanding. He stood on the station platform staring steadily after us, and as long as we had sight of him in the thick, bitter dust, the Look held.

If this were a story merely, or a story of Franklin Challoner, it would end there. He never thought of us again, you may depend, except to thank his stars for getting so lightly off, and to go on in the security of his success to other episodes from which he returned as scatheless.

But I found out in a very few days that whether it was to take rank as an incident or an event in Netta Saybrick's life depended on whether or not I said anything about it. Nobody had taken any notice of her day's ride to Posada. Say brick came home in about ten days, and Netta seemed uncommonly glad to see him, as if in the preoccupation of his presence she found a solace for her fears.

But from the day of our return she had evinced an extraordinary liking for my company. She would be running in and out of the house at all hours, offering to help me with my sewing or to stir up a cake, kindly offices that had to be paid in kind; and if I slipped into the neighbors' on an errand, there a moment after would come Netta. Very soon it became clear to me that she was afraid of what I might tell. So long as she had me under her immediate eye she could be sure I was not taking away her character, but when I was not, she must have suffered horribly. I might have told, too, by the woman's code; she was really not respectable, and we made a great deal of that in Maverick. I might refuse to have anything to do with her and justified myself explaining why.

But Netta was not sure how much I knew, and could not risk betrayal by a plea. She had, too, the natural reticence of the villager, and though she must have been aching for news of Doctor Challoner, touch of him, the very sound of his name, she rarely ever mentioned it, but grew strained and thinner; watching, watching.

If that incident was known, Netta would have been ostracized and Saybrick might have divorced her. And I was going dumb with amazement to discover that nothing had come of it, nothing *could* come of it so long as I kept still. It was a deadly sin, as I had been taught, as I believed - of damnable potentiality; and as long as nobody told it was as if it had never been, as if that look of Challoner's had really the power as it had the seeming of absolving her from all soil and stain.

I cannot now remember if I was ever tempted to tell on Netta Saybrick, but I know with the obsession of that look upon my soul I never did. And in the mean time, from being so much in each other's company, Netta and I became very good friends. That was why, a little more than a year afterward, she chose to have me with her when her second child was born. In Maverick we did things for one another that in more sophisticated communities go to the service of paid attendants. That was the time when the suspicion that had lain at the bottom of Netta's shallow eyes whenever she looked at me went out of them forever.

It was along about midnight and the worst yet to come. I sat holding Netta's hands, and beyond in the room where the lamp was, the doctor lifted Saybrick through his stressful hour with cribbage and toddy. I could see the gleam of the light on Saybrick's red, hairy hands, a driller's hands, and whenever a sound came from the inner room, the uneasy lift of his shoulders and the twitching of his lip; then the doctor pushed the whiskey over toward him and jovially dealt the cards anew.

Netta, tossing on her pillow, came into range with Saybrick's blunt profile outlined against the cheaply papered wall, and I suppose her husband's distress was good to her to see. She looked at him a long time quietly.

"Henry's a good man," she said at last.

"Yes," I said; and then she turned to me narrowly with the expiring spark of anxious cunning in her eyes.

"And I've been a good wife to him," said she. It was half a challenge. And I, trapped by the hour, became a fakir in my turn, called instantly on all my soul and answered with the Look - "Everybody knows that, Netta" - held on steadily until the spark went out. However I had done it I could not tell, but I saw the trouble go out of the woman's soul as the lids drooped, and with it out of my own heart the last of the virtuous resentment of the untempted. I had really forgiven her; how then was it possible for the sin to rise up and trouble her more? Mind you, I grew up in a church that makes a great deal of the forgiveness of sins and signifies it by a tremendous particularity about behavior, and the most I had learned of the efficient exercise of forgiveness was from the worst man I had ever known.

About an hour before dawn, when a wind began to stir, and out on the mesa the coyotes howled returning from the hunt, stooping to tuck the baby in her arms, I felt Netta's lips brush against my hand.

"You've been mighty good to me," she said.

Well - if I were pushed for it, I should think it worth mentioning - but I am not so sure.

When Tennessee, after about sixty years of prospecting, grub-staking, and days' wages, had made a little strike, he declared himself done with desertness, and of a mind to go down to the city to some recently developed connections and heirs, to be properly taken care of for the rest of his years. That was along in the beginning of winter, when interest narrowed to watching the snow-line approach and recede along the flank of the Sierras, and the undertaking was accounted to him for wisdom. And about two months later, when I was out looking mesaward for the pale tinge of the freshening sage that, however fast you may seek toward it, is no more to be come up with than the mirage, suddenly across my prospect bulked the large, lumbering figure of Tennessee. What he said was that in the city he could never step out of the door but there was a house right bung up against his eyes.

"A man," said Tennessee, "don't have no chance to stretch his vision."

But when the Rev. William Calvin Gains came down fresh from his seminary somewhere about Oakland to awaken, in the best imitation of a popular city preacher he could manage, our interest in spiritual things, he made just the opposite mistake of not understanding that here the vision stretches beyond the boundary of sense and things. Though the desert has had a reputation in times past for the making of religious leaders, it is no field for converts. Judge how a conventional, pew-fed religion would flourish in the presence of what I am about to relate to you.

Chapter Ten - The Pocket-Hunter's Story

THE crux of this story for the Pocket-Hunter was that he had known the two men, Mac and Creelman, before they came into it; known them, in fact, in the beginning of that mutual distrust which grew out of an earlier friendliness into one of those expansive enmities which in the spined and warted humanity of the camps have as ready an acceptance as the devoted partnerships of which Wells Bassit furnished the pre-eminent example. It was, he believed, in some such relationship their acquaintance had begun, and from which they now drew the sustenance of those separate devils of hate that, nesting in corrosive hollows of their hosts, rose to froth and rage, each at the mere intimation of a merit in the other.

No one knew what the turn of the screw had been that set them gnashing, but it was supposed, on no better evidence, perhaps, than that such trouble is at the bottom of most quarrels in the camps, to have been about a mine. The final crisis, the very memory of which seemed to hold for him a moment of recurrent, hair-lifting horror, was known by the Pocket-Hunter, and by some of the others, to have been brought on by an Indian woman down Parrimint-way.

She was Mac's woman; though, except as being his, he was not thought to set particular store by her. He used to leave her in his cabin while he was off in the Hills for a three weeks' *pasear;* but the tacit admission of an Indian woman as no fit subject for white men to fight over forbade his being put to the ordinary provocation on account of her. Therefore, when Creelman projected his offence, which was to excite in his enemy the desire for killing without providing him with a sufficient excuse, there was a vague notion moving in the heavy fibre of his mind that there was a species of humor in what he was about to do. But he would probably not have gone on to Tres Piños and told of it, if he had known how soon it was to come to Mac's ears.

This, you understand, was long after their grudge had climbed by inconsiderable occasions to the point where Mac had several times offered to kill Creelman on no motion but the pleasure of being rid of his company.

Mac was a sickly man, and by that, and his having had the worst of it in their earlier encounters, his rage so much the more possessed him that, when he had come back to his cabin and the Indian woman had told him her story, he was able by that mere spur of a possession trifled with to take the short leap from intent to performance at a bound. There was no such bodily leap possible, of course; he had to trudge the whole of one day on foot to Tres Piños, an old weakness battling with his rage. He was one of those illy-furnished souls whom the wilderness despoils most completely - hair, beard, and skin of him burned to one sandy sallowness, the eyelashes of no color, the voice of no timbre, more or less stiffened at the joints by the poison of leaded ores, his very name shorn of its distinguishing syllable; no more of him left, in fact, than would serve as a vehicle for hating Creelman. When he came to Tres Piños and learned that the other had gone on from there, nobody would tell him where, the rage of bafflement threw him into some kind of a fit, and blood gushed from his nose and mouth.

All this the Pocket-Hunter was possessed of when he set out shortly after with his pack and burros, prospecting toward the Dry Creek district, where in due time he crossed the trail of Shorty Wells and Long Tom Bassit. There was no particular reason why Wells should have been called Shorty, except that Long Tom was of a stature to give to any average man in his vicinity a title to that adjective. Further than that he gave no other warrant to the virtues, aptitudes, propensities with which Shorty credited him, than the negative one of not denying them. In camps where they were known the opinion gained ground that there was very little to Long Tom but his size and his amiability, which was remarked upon, but that Shorty, having discovered this creditable baggage in his own pack, had laid it to Bassit, not being able to say else how he came by it; but there they were, as inveterate a pair of partners as the camps ever bred, owning to no greater satisfaction than just to be abroad in the hills together following the Golden Hope; and there on a day between Dry Creek and Denman's the Pocket-Hunter found them.

The way he came to tell me about it was this. I had laid by for a nooning under the quaking-asp by Peterscreek on the trail from Tunawai, and found him before me with his head under one of those woven shelters of living boughs which the sheep-herders leave in that country, and he moved out to make room for me in its hand's-breadth of shade.

Understand, there was no more shade to be got there. Straight before us went the meagre sands; to every yard or so of space its foot-high, sapless shrub. Somewhere at the back of us lifted, out of a bank of pinkish-violet mist, sierras white and airy. Eastward where the earth sagged on its axis, in some dreary, beggared sleep, pale, wispish clouds went up. Now and then to no wind the quaking-asps clattered their dry bones of leaves.

We had been talking, the Pocket-Hunter and I, of that curious obsession of travel by which the mind, pressing on in the long, open trail ahead of the dragging desert pace, seems often to develop a capacity for going on alone in it, so that it becomes involved in one sliding picture, as it were, of what is ahead and what at hand, until, when the body stops for necessary rest and food, it is impossible to say if it is here where it halted, or there where the mind possessed. I had said that this accounted to me not only for the extraordinary feats of endurance in desert travel, but for the great difficulty prospectors have in relocating places they have marked, so mazed they are by that mixed aspect of strangeness and familiarity that every district wears, which, long before it has been entered by the body, has been appraised by the eye of the mind.

"But suppose," said the Pocket-Hunter, "it really does go on by itself?"

"And where," I wished to know, "would be the witness to that, unless it brought back a credible report of what it had seen?"

"Or done," suggested the Pocket-Hunter, "what it set out to do. That would clinch it, I fancy."

"But the mind can only take notice," I protested. "It can't *do* anything without its body."

"Or another one," suggested the Pocket-Hunter.

"Ah," said I, "tell me the story."

It was, went on the Pocket-Hunter, after he had told me all that I have set down about the four men who made the story, about nine of the morning when he came to Dry Creek on the way to Jawbone cañon, and the day was beginning to curl up and smoke along the edges with the heat, rocking with the motion of it, and water of mirage rolling like quick-silver in the hollows. What the Pocket-Hunter said exactly was that it was a morning in May, but it comes to the same thing. He had just come out of the wash by Cactus Flat when he was aware of a man chasing about in the heat fog, and making out to want something more than common. Even as early as that in the incident the Pocket-Hunter thought he had encoun-tered some faint, floating films from that coil of inexplicable dreadfulness in which he was so soon to find himself involved, and yet he was not sure that it might not have been chiefly in the extraordinary manner of the man's approach, seeing him caught up in the mirage, drawn out and dwarfed again, "like some kind of human accordion,'* said the Pocket-Hunter, and now rolled toward him with limbs grotesquely multiplied in a river of mist.

Presently, however, he got the man between him and the sun, in such a way that he was able to make out it was himself who was wanted, and when he had slewed the burros round to come up to him, he could see plainly who it was, and it was Wells. It was altogether so unusual a cir-cumstance to find Shorty Wells anywhere out of eyeshot of Tom Bassit that it was not reassuring, and Shorty himself was so sensible of it that almost before any greeting passed, he had let out with certain swallow-ings of the throat that Tom was dead.

It appeared the two of them had come over Tinpah two days before, and Bassit, who had a weakness of the heart that made high places a menace to him, had accomplished the Pass apparently in good order. But when they had taken the immense drop that carries one from the crest of Tinpah to Dry Creek like a bucket in a shaft, something had gone sudden-ly, irretrievably wrong. There had been a half collapse at the foot of the trail, and a complete one a few miles back on the trail to Denman's, to-ward which they had turned in extremity. Tom had suffered agonizingly, so that if there had been any place nearer from which help might con-ceivably have come, Shorty could not have left him to go and fetch it; and along about the hour which the Indians call, all in one word, the bluish-light-of-dawn, Tom had died.

All the way back to camp, after he had met the Pocket-Hunter, Shorty kept arguing with himself as to whether, if he had done the one thing or had not done the other, it would have been better for poor Tom, and the Pocket-Hunter assuring him for his comfort that it would not, keeping back, by some native stroke of sympathy, what he had lately heard at Tres

Piños - that Creelman had a cabin in the Jawbone, and was living in it what time Mac was camping on his trail. It was no farther from the foot of Tinpah than they had come toward Denman's, but in the opposite direction, and from their not turning there it seemed likely they had not heard of it - kinder if Shorty might never come to know, seeing he had not known it in time to be of use to Tom. And this was a point the Pocket-Hunter was presently to make sure of, that neither Shorty nor Long Tom was acquainted with the location of the cabin, nor with Mac nor Creelman by sight.

As it was, he made the most of comforting Shorty for having stayed by his partner to the last.

"I never left him till he croaked," Shorty told him. "It was along toward morning he went quiet, and just as I was goin' for to cover him with the blanket, he croaked - and I come away."

There was that touch of dread in him which ever the figure of death excites in simple minds, which, perhaps as much as the wish to bring help to the burial, had turned him from the body of the friend who was, and now kept his eyes fixed persistently upon the ground as they came back to it across the flat, which here, made smooth in shining, leprous patches of alkali, presented no screen to the disordered camp higher than the sickly pickle-weed about its borders. The Pocket-Hunter, therefore, as they came on toward the place where from two crossed sticks of Shorty's fire a thin point of flame wavered upward, had time for wondering greatly at what he saw, which was so little what he had been led to expect there that he had not found yet any warrant for mentioning it, when Shorty, gathering himself toward what he had to face, lifting up his eyes, let out a kind of howl and ran.

The Pocket-Hunter said he did not know how soon Shorty grasped the fact, which he himself perceived with his eyes some time before his intelligence took hold of it, that the body lying doubled on the sand some yards from the empty bed was not the same that Shorty had left stiffening under the blanket. He thought they must have both taken account of it at the same time, and been stricken dumb by the sheer horror of it, for he could not remember a word spoken by either of them, between Shorty's sharp yell of astonishment and the time when they took it by the shoulders and turned it to the sun.

The limbs were still lax enough with recent life to settle slowly as they stirred the body; there were no wounds upon it, but blood had gushed freely from the nose and mouth. It was a smallish man of no particular color or complexion, with that slight distortion of the joints common in a country of leaded ores. By these marks, as they discovered themselves in the sharp light, the Pocket-Hunter was able to identify him as a man

Shorty had never seen, last heard of at Tres Piños, where he had fallen by rage into some such seizure as had apparently overtaken him upon the trail. That he should be here at all, and in such a case as this, was sufficiently horrifying, but it was nothing to the appalling wonder as to what had become of Tom.

There was the impress of his body upon the bed, and the blanket, shed in loose folds across the foot, now lifted a little and buoyed by the wind, and in all the wide day nothing to hide a man, except where, miles behind, the sheer bulk of Tinpah was split by shadowy gulfs of cañons. Shorty was, for the time, fairly tottering in his mind. He would pry foolishly about the camp, getting back by quick turns and pounces to the stretched body on the sand, as though in the interim it might have recovered from its extraordinary illusion and become the body of his friend again. By degrees the Pocket-Hunter constrained him to piece out the probable circumstance.

They had to begin, of course, with Tom's not being dead, and to go on from that to the previous fact of Mac working his poor body over the long stretches between Tres Piños and the Jawbone, where he must have learned that Creelman was hiding. Well, he *had* a poor body, and it must have given out under him just as he arrived in camp, very shortly after Shorty had left it, and, over-ridden by his errand, had persuaded Long Tom, then recovering from his trance or swoon, to rise and go on with it.

"To kill Creelman! Tom?"

Shorty's imagination flagged visibly in the eye of Tom's huge amiability, but the Pocket-Hunter came around triumphantly.

"Well, he went!"

"But he couldn't have," Shorty put forward, hopefully, as if any bar to his partner's leaving the camp might somehow result in proving him still there. "He hadn't stood on his feet for twenty-four hours, and suffered something awful. Besides, he didn't know there was a cabin; if he had, I'd have gone there yesterday."

"Mac would have told him, of course."

Shorty drooped dejectedly before a supposition that, however large the hope it entailed of finding his partner still in the flesh, afforded no relief to the incontrovertible persistence of evidence in his own mind. "But he croaked, I tell you - they're dead when they croak, ain't they?"

Whatever was said to that was said by the zt-z-z-t of desert flies punctuating the heavy heat. At the sound of it little beads of sweat broke out on Shorty's face.

"Look a-here," he brought out, finally, "if this other fellow, Mac here, was as bad off as you say, why didn't Tom go to him; kind of ease him off like? What for did he go off and leave him crumpled up like that?"

"He wouldn't have died until after Tom left, Mac wouldn't," the Pocket-Hunter reminded him. "What makes you so sure?"

"Tom never walked none after we struck camp." Shorty was secure of his ground here. "And there's no tracks of him except where he came in alongside of me - and goin' out - *there!*" The print of Tom's large feet had turned toward the Jawbone. "Besides," he returned to it with anxiety, "what would he go to Creelman's for?"

This was a point, and the Pocket-Hunter took as much time as was necessary to shroud the dead man in Tom's blanket to consider it. He found this at last:

"Tom," he said, "was a peaceable man?"

"None peaceabler," admitted Tom's partner.

"Well, then, when he found this little –" (the adjective checked out of respect to the object of it being as he was) "Mac here so set on killing, he thought it no more than right to get on ahead and give Creelman a hint of what was coming to him."

This being so much what might have been expected of Tom, it appeared insensibly to give greater plausibility to the whole occasion. It left them for the moment free to set out on Tom's trail with almost a movement of naturalness. It lasted, however, only long enough to see them into the steady, flowing stride of desert travel; the recurrence of that motion, perhaps, set up again in Shorty's mind the consciousness of loss in which it had some two hours earlier begun, and the consideration of mere practical details, such as the distance from the camp to Creelman's, swept back to the full the conviction of unreality.

Looking ahead at the long trudge between them and the mouth of the cañon, where in that clear light, on that level mesa, no man could have moved unespied by them, where, in fact, no man at that moment was moving, he broke out in a kind of exasperated wail:

"But he couldn't have, I tell you; he couldn't have walked it...He was dead, I tell you...He croaked and I covered him up...."

It became momentarily clearer to the Pocket-Hunter that unless they came soon, behind some screening weed, in some unguessed hollow, upon Long Tom's huddled body, collapsed in the recurrent weakness of his disorder, so to restore the event to reasonableness, he must find himself swamped again in the horror of the inexplicable, out of which they had been speciously pulled by the Pocket-Hunter's argument.

It was not until they came to the loose shale and sand at the mouth of the cañon that Shorty reverted again to the form of his amazement.

"Did you notice," said he, "anything queer about Tom's tracks?"

"Queer, how?"

"Well - different?"

"Like he thought he had a game leg?" suggested the Pocket-Hunter.

"Well, he hadn't...but the other man...back yonder...*he* had a game leg."

"Shorty! Shorty!" the Pocket-Hunter fairly begged. "You ain't...you mustn't...let your mind run on them things!"

"Well, he had," persisted Wells. His voice clicked with dryness, trailed off whispering. It seemed to the Pocket-Hunter, suddenly, that the twenty steps or so between the man so certainly dead in his tracks on one side the fire back there, and the supposedly dead arising in his on the other, had swelled to immeasurable space. It was then there came into his mind the remainder of that singular obsession of the trail in the notice of which our conversation had begun. He saw on the instant Mac inching out from Tres Piños on his unmatched poor legs, his hate riding far before him, blown forward by some devil's blast, tugging at him like a kite at its ballast, lifting him past incredible stretches of hot sand and cutting stone, until it dropped him there. He wrenched his mind away from that by an effort, and fixed it on the pale pine-colored square of Creelman's cabin, where it began to show in the shadowy gulf of the cañon.

The door was open and the curtains of the two small windows on either side half drawn against a glare which would have been gone from that side of the cañon more than an hour ago. Here, as they halted to take notice of it, some expiring gasps of bluish smoke from Creelman's breakfast fire went up from the tin chimney against the basalt wall. As they came near they observed a large flaccid hand hanging out over the sill. What they made out further was Creelman's body, extended face downward, barring the door. A small lizard tic-tacked on the unpainted boards across the hand that did not start at it, and disappeared into the shadow of the room, where, as if this intrusion gave them leave to look, they perceived among the broken plates and disordered furniture a broken pack-stick, Creelman's knife, open and blooded the figure of Long Tom, half propped against the footboard of the bunk, dropping weakly from a wound. It was Tom, though over his face as it leered up at them was spread a strange new expressiveness, such a superficial and furtive change as frivolous passers-by will add sometimes to the face of a poster with pencil touches, provoking to half startled laughter; plain enough to have shocked them back, even as against the witness of clothes and hair and features, from the instant's recognition, to produce in them an amazement, momentary, yet long enough for the dying man to take note of them unfriendlily, and to have addressed himself to the Pocket-Hunter.

"Came to see the fight, did you? It's damned well over ...but I did for him ...the ___, ___, ___!" His body sank visibly with the stream of curses.

But the faith of Shorty was proof even against this. He had cleared the body of Creelman at a stride, and was on his knees beside his partner, crying very simply.

"Oh, Tom, Tom," he begged, "you never done it? Say you never done it, pardner, say you never!"

"Aw, who the hell are you?" The lewd eyes rolled up at him, he gave two or three long gasps which ended in a short choking gurgle, the body started slightly, and dropped.

"Come away, Shorty, he's croaked," said the Pocket-Hunter not unkindly; but Shorty knelt on there, crying quietly as he watched the dead man's features settle and stiffen to the likeness of his friend.

Chapter Eleven - The Readjustment

Emma Jeffries had been dead and buried three days. The sister who had come to the funeral had taken Emma's child away with her, and the house was swept and aired; then, when it seemed there was least occasion for it, Emma came back. The neighbor woman who had nursed her was the first to know it. It was about seven of the evening in a mellow gloom: the neighbor woman was sitting on her own stoop with her arms wrapped in her apron, and all at once she found herself going along the street under an urgent sense that Emma needed her. She was halfway down the block before she recollected that this was impossible, for Mrs. Jeffries was dead and buried; but as soon as she came opposite the house she was aware of what had happened. It was all open to the summer air; except that it was a little neater, not otherwise than the rest of the street. It was quite dark; but the presence of Emma Jeffries streamed from it and betrayed it more than a candle. It streamed out steadily across the garden, and even as it reached her, mixed with the smell of the damp mignonette, the neighbor woman owned to herself that she had always known Emma would come back.

"A sight stranger if she wouldn't," thought the woman who had nursed her. "She wasn't ever one to throw off things easily."

Emma Jeffries had taken death as she had taken everything in life, hard. She had met it with the same bright, surface competency that she had presented to the squalor of the encompassing desertness, to the insuperable commonness of Sim Jeffries, to the affliction of her crippled child; and the intensity of her wordless struggle against it had caught the attention of the townspeople and held it in a shocked curious awe. She was so long a-dying, lying there in that little low house, hearing the abhorred footsteps going about her rooms and the vulgar procedure of the community encroach upon her like the advances of the sand wastes on an unwatered field. For Emma had always wanted things different, wanted them with a fury of intentness that implied offensiveness in things as they were. And the townspeople had taken offence, the more so because she was not to be surprised in any inaptitude for their own kind of success. Do what you could, you could never catch Emma Jeffries in a wrapper after three o'clock in the afternoon. And she would never talk about the child - in a country where so little ever happened that even trouble was a godsend if it gave you something to talk about. It was reported that she did not even talk to Sim. But there the common resentment got back at her. If she had thought to effect anything with Sim Jeffries against the be-numbing spirit of the place, the evasive hopefulness, the large sense of leisure that ungirt the loins, if she still hoped somehow to get away with him to some place for which by her dress, by her manner, she seemed forever and unassailably fit, it was foregone that nothing would come of it. They knew Sim Jeffries better than that. Yet so vivid had been the force of her wordless dissatisfaction that when the fever took her and she went down like a pasteboard figure in the damp, the wonder was that nothing toppled with her. And, as if she too had felt herself indispensable, Emma Jeffries had come back.

The neighbor woman crossed the street, and as she passed the far corner of the garden, Jeffries spoke to her. He had been standing, she did not know how long a time, behind the syringa-bush, and moved even with her along the fence until they came to the gate. She could see in the dusk that before speaking he wet his lips with his tongue.

"She's in there," he said, at last.

"Emma?"

He nodded. "I been sleeping at the store since - but I thought I'd be more comfortable - as soon as I opened the door there she was."

"Did you see her?"

"No."

"How do you know, then?"

"Don't you know?"

The neighbor felt there was nothing to say to that.

"Come in," he whispered, huskily. They slipped by the rose-tree and the wistaria, and sat down on the porch at the side. A door swung inward behind them. They felt the Presence in the dusk beating like a pulse.

"What do you think she wants?" said Jeffries. "Do you reckon it's the boy?"

"Like enough."

"He's better off with his aunt. There was no one here to take care of him like his mother wanted." He raised his voice unconsciously with a note of justification, addressing the room behind.

"I am sending fifty dollars a month," he said; "he can go with the best of them."

He went on at length to explain all the advantage that was to come to the boy from living at Pasadena, and the neighbor woman bore him out in it.

"He was glad to go," urged Jeffries to the room. "He said it was what his mother would have wanted."

They were silent then a long time, while the Presence seemed 'to swell upon them and encroached upon the garden.

Finally, "I gave Ziegler the order for the monument yesterday, "Jeffries threw out, appeasingly. "It's to cost three hundred and fifty."

The Presence stirred. The neighbor thought she could fairly see the controlled tolerance with which Emma Jeffries endured the evidence of Sim's ineptitudes.

They sat on helplessly without talking after that until the woman's husband came to the fence and called her.

"Don't go," begged Sim.

"Hush," she said. "Do you want all the town to know? You had naught but good from Emma living, and no call to expect harm from her now. It's natural she should come back - if - if she was lonesome like - in - the place where she's gone to."

"Emma wouldn't come back to this place," Jeffries protested, "without she wanted something."

"Well, then, you've got to find out," said the neighbor woman.

All the next day she saw, whenever she passed the house, that Emma was still there. It was shut and barred, but the Presence lurked behind the folded blinds and fumbled at the doors. When it was night and the moths began in the columbine under the windows, it went out and walked in the garden.

Jeffries was waiting at the gate when the neighbor woman came. He sweated with helplessness in the warm dusk, and the Presence brooded upon them like an apprehension that grows by being entertained.

"She wants something," he appealed, "but I can't make out what. Emma knows she is welcome to everything I've got. Everybody knows I've been a good provider."

The neighbor woman remembered suddenly the only time she had ever drawn close to Emma Jeffries touching the boy. They had sat up with it together all one night in some childish ailment, and she had ventured a question. "What does his father think?" And Emma had turned her a white, hard face of surpassing dreariness.

"I don't know," she admitted, "he never says."

"There's more than providing," suggested the neighbor woman.

"Yes. There's feeling...but she had enough to do to put up with me. I had no call to be troubling her with such." He left off to mop his forehead, and began again.

"Feelings!" he said, "there's times a man gets so wore out with feelings he doesn't have them any more."

He talked, and presently it grew clear to the woman that he was voiding all the stuff of his life, as if he had sickened on it and was now done.

It was a little soul knowing itself and not good to see. What was singular was that the Presence left off walking in the garden, came and caught like a gossamer on the ivy-tree, swayed by the breath of his broken sentences. He talked, and the neighbor woman saw him for once as he saw himself and Emma, snared and floundering in an inexplicable unhappiness. He had been disappointed, too. She had never relished the man he was, and it made him ashamed. That was why he had never gone away, lest he should make her ashamed among her own kind. He was her husband, he could not help that though he was sorry for it. But he could keep the offence where least was made of it. And there was a child - she had wanted a child; but even then he had blundered begotten a cripple upon her. He blamed himself utterly, searched out the roots of his youth for the answer to that, until the neighbor woman flinched to hear him. But the Presence stayed.

He had never talked to his wife about the child. How should he? There was the fact - the advertisement of his incompetence. And she had never talked to him. That was the one blessed and unassailable memory; that she had spread silence like a balm over his hurt. In return for it he had never gone away. He had resisted her that he might save her from showing among her own kind how poor a man he was. With every word of this ran the fact of his love for her - as he had loved her, with all the stripes of clean and uncleanness. He bared himself as a child without knowing; and the Presence stayed. The talk trailed off at last to the commonplaces of consolation between the retchings of his spirit. The Presence lessened and streamed toward them on the wind of the garden. When it touched them like the warm air of noon that lies sometimes in hollow places after nightfall, the neighbor woman rose and went away.

The next night she did not wait for him. When a rod outside the town - it was a very little one – the burrowing owls *whoo-whooed*, she hung up her apron and went to talk with Emma Jeffries. The Presence was there, drawn in, lying close. She found the key between the wistaria and the first pillar of the porch, but as soon as she opened the door she felt the chill that might be expected by one intruding on Emma Jeffries in her own house.

"'The Lord is my shepherd,'" said the neighbor woman; it was the first religious phrase that occurred to her; then she said the whole of the psalm and after that a hymn. She had come in through the door and stood with her back to it and her hand upon the knob. Everything was just as Mrs. Jeffries had left it, with the waiting air of a room kept for company.

"Em," she said, boldly, when the chill had abated a little before the sacred words. "Em Jeffries, I've got something to say to you. And you've got to hear," she added with firmness, as the white curtains stirred duskily at the window. "You wouldn't be talked to about your troubles when...you were here before; and we humored you. But now there is Sim to be thought of. I guess you heard what you came for last night, and got good of it. Maybe it would have been better if Sim had said things all along instead of hoarding them in his heart, but any way he has said them now. And what I want to say is, if you was staying on with the hope of hearing it again, you'd be making a mistake. You was an uncommon woman, Emma Jeffries, and there didn't none of us understand you very well, nor do you justice maybe; but Sim is only a common man, and I understand him because I'm that way myself. And if you think he'll be opening his heart to you every night, or be any different from what he's always been on account of what's happened, that's a mistake too...and in a little while, if you stay, it will be as bad as it always was...Men are like that....You'd better go now while there's understanding between you." She stood staring into the darkling room that seemed suddenly full of turbulence and denial. It seemed to beat upon her and take her breath, but she held on.

"You've got to go...Em...and I'm going to stay until you do." She said this with finality, and then began again.

"'The Lord is nigh unto them that are of a broken heart,'" and repeated the passage to the end. Then as the Presence sank before it. "You better go, Emma," persuasively, and again after an interval:

"'He shall deliver thee in six troubles, yea, in seven shall no evil touch thee.'"

...The Presence gathered itself and was still. She could make out that it stood over against the opposite corner by the gilt easel with the crayon portrait of the child.

..."'For thou shalt forget thy misery. Thou shalt remember it as waters that are past,'" concluded the neighbor woman, as she heard Jeffries on the gravel outside. What the Presence had wrought upon him in the night was visible in his altered mien. He looked more than anything else to be in need of sleep. He had eaten his sorrow, and that was the end of it - as it is with men.

"I came to see if there was anything I could do for you," said the woman, neighborly, with her hand upon the door.

"I don't know as there is," said he; "I'm much obliged, but I don't know as there is."

"You see," whispered the woman over her shoulder, "not even to me." She felt the tug of her heart as the Presence swept past her.

The neighbor went out after that and walked in the ragged street, past the school-house, across the creek below the town, out by the fields, over the headgate, and back by the town again. It was full nine of the clock when she passed the Jeffries house. It looked, except for being a little neater, not other than the rest of the street. The door was open and the lamp was lit; she saw Jeffries, black against it. He sat reading in a book, like a man at ease in his own house.

Chapter Twelve - Bitterness of Women

LOUIS CHABOT was sitting under the fig-tree in her father's garden at Tres Piños when he told Marguerita Dupré that he could not love her. This sort of thing happened so often to Louis that he did it very well and rather enjoyed it, for he was one of those before whom women bloomed instinctively and preened themselves; and that Marguerita loved him very much was known not only to Louis but to all Tres Piños.

It was bright mid-afternoon, and there was no sound in Dupré's garden louder than the dropping of ripe figs and the drip of the hydrant under the Castilian roses. A mile out of town Chabot's flock dozed on their feet, with their heads under one another's bellies, and his herders dozed on the ground, with their heads under the plaited tops of the sage. Old Dupré sat out in front of his own front yard with a handkerchief over his face, and slept very soundly. Chabot finished his claret to the last drop (it was excellent claret, this of Dupré's), turned the tumbler upside down, sat back in his chair, and explained to Marguerita point by point why he did not love her.

Marguerita leaned her fat arms on the table, wrapped in her blue reboza; it was light blue, and she was too dark for it; but it was such a pretty color. She leaned forward, looking steadily and quietly at Louis, because she was afraid if she so much as let her lids droop the tears would come, and if she smiled her lips would quiver. Marguerita felt that she had not invited this, neither had she known how to avoid it. She would have given anything to have told Louis to his face that he need not concern himself so much on her account, as she was not the least interested in him; she had called on all her pride to that end, but nothing came.

She Leaned Forward, Looking Steadily and Quietly at Louis

She was a good girl, Louis told her, such as, if she had pleased him, he would gladly have married. She was a very good girl, and she understood about sheep. *Tres-bien!* Old Dupré had taught her that; but she lacked a trifle - a nuance - but everything where love is concerned, *l'art d'être désiré*, explained the little Frenchman; for though he was only a sheepherder of Lost Borders, if he had been a boulevardier he could not have been more of a Frenchman nor less of a cad. He leaned back in his chair with the air of having delivered himself very well.

"Salty Bill loves me," ventured Marguerita.

"Eh, Bill!" Louis looked hurt, for though he frequently disposed of his ladies in this negligent fashion, he did not care to have them snapped up so quickly. Marguerita felt convicted of *lèse-majesté* by the look, and hastened to reassure him that she cared nothing whatever for Salty Bill. It was a false move, and she knew it as soon as it was done; but she could not bear to have Louis look at her like that, and Marguerita had never in her life learned the good of pretending. Chabot poured him another glass of claret, and returned to his point.

There was Suzon Moynier, he explained. Such an eye as Suzon had! there was a spark for you! And an ankle! more lovers than few had been won by an ankle. Marguerita, under cover of the table, drew her feet together beneath her skirts. Her ankles were thick, and there was no disguising it.

"So it is Suzon you love?"

"Eh," said the herder, "that is as may be. I have loved many women." Then perhaps because the particular woman did not matter so much as that there should be womanhood, and perhaps because he could no more help it than she could help being wondrously flooded by it, he threw her a look from the tail of his eye and such a smile as drew all the blood from her heart, bent above her, brushing her hair with his lips in such a lingering tenderness of farewell, that though he had just told her she was not to be loved, the poor girl was not sure but he was beginning to love her. Women suffered things like that from Louis Chabot, each being perfectly sure she was the only one, and perhaps, like Marguerita, finding it worth while to be made to suffer if it could be done so exquisitely.

Marguerita was only half French herself, old Dupré having married her mother, Senorita Carrasco, who was only half a senorita, since, in fact, most people in Tres Piños were a little this or that, with no chance for name-calling. Dupre had been a herder of sheep, risen to an owner whom the Desert had bitten. The natural consequence was that when he was old, instead of returning to France, he had married Marguerita's mother, and settled down in Tres Piños to live on the interest of his money.

It was a fact that his daughter had at heart all the fire and tenderness that promised in Suzon's glance; but of what use to Louis, Chabot that she had a soul warm and alight if no glow of it suffused her cheek and no spark of it drew him in her eye. She was swarthy and heavy of face; she had no figure, which means she had a great deal too much of it, and there was a light shadow, like a finger-smudge, on her upper lip. Not that the girl did not have her good points. She could cook, that was the French strain in her father; she could dance, that was Castilian from her mother; and such as she was Salty Bill wanted her. Bill drove an eighteen-mule team for the borax works and was seven times a better man than Chabot, but she would have no more of him than Louis would have cf her. She continued to say her prayers regularly, and told Tia Juana, who reproached her with losing a good marriage, that she believed yet the saints would give her the desire of her heart, whereat Tia Juana pitied her.

Chabot brought his sheep up from the spring shearing at Bakersfield each year, and made three loops about Tres Piños, so that it brought him to the town about once in three months to replenish his supplies, and the only reason there was not a new object of his attentions each time was that there were not girls enough, for Chabot's taste required them young, pretty, and possessed of the difficult art of being desired. Therefore, he had time to keep hope alive in Marguerita with the glint of his flattering eyes and the trick of his flattering lips, which was such very common coin with him that he did not quite know himself how free he was with it. And after old Dupré died and his daughter inherited his house and the interest on his money, she was enough of a figure in Tres Piños to make a little attention worth while, even though she had a smudge of black on her upper lip and no art but that of being faithful. She lived in the house under the figtree with old Tia Juana for a companion, and was much respected. She was said to have more clothes than anybody, though they never became her.

Marguerita kept a candle burning before the saints and another in her heart for the handsome little herder who went on making love to ladies and being loved by them for three years. Then the saints took a hand in his affairs, though, of course, it did not look that way to Louis.

He was sleeping out on Black Mountain in the spring of the year with his flock. The herder whose business it was to have done that was at Tres Piños on a two days' leave, confessing himself, and getting a nice, jolly little claret drunk. Somewhere up in the blown lava-holes of Black Mountain there was a bear with two cubs, who had said to them, bear fashion: "Come down to the flock with me tonight, and I will show you how killing is done. There will be dogs there and men; but do not be afraid, I will see to it that they do not hurt you."

Along about the time Orion's sword sloped down the west, Chabot heard their gruntled noises and the scurry of the flock. Chabot was not a coward; perhaps because he knew that in general bears are; he got up and laid about him with his staff. This he never would have done if he had known about the cubs; he trod on the foot of one in the dark, and the bear mother heard it. She came lumbering up in the soft blackness and took Chabot in her arms.

Toward four of the next afternoon, the herder coming back, still very merry and very comfortable in his mind, found a maimed, bleeding thing by the water-hole that moaned and babbled. One of its arms was gone to the elbow, its face was laid open, and long, red gashes lay along its sides and down one thigh. After a while, when he had washed away the blood and dust, he discovered that this thing was Chabot. The herder laid it as tenderly as he could on the camp burro and took it in to Tres Piños. If there was any question of the propriety of the care of Chabot falling to Marguerita Dupré, it counted for nothing against the fact that nobody was found willing to do it in her stead, and Marguerita was very discreet. Tia Juana was put in charge of the sick-room, and Marguerita gave her whole soul to the cooking.

And if any question had arisen later when Chabot began to hobble about with a crutch under his good arm, and his sleeve pinned up where the other had been, he put an end to it by marrying her. He was thought to have done very well in this, since he could get no more good of himself; and since Marguerita wanted him it was a handsome way of paying her, but there had something gone before that. Tia Juana had been careful there should be no scrap of a mirror about when Chabot began to slip his bandages, and perhaps he had not had the courage to ask for it; certainly there had been no change in Marguerita's face for any change she saw in him. And the day that he knew the thing he was, he asked her to marry him. He had slipped out into the street for the first time, wearying a little of the solicitations of the two women, and, to say truth, wholly misinterpreting Marguerita's reasons for screening him so much from the public gaze, for she, poor girl, when he had asked her, could only tell him that he was quite as handsome as ever in her eyes. He felt the pleasant tingle of the air and the sun and the smell of grapes and dropping leafage from the little arbors of Tres Piños, and at the turn of the street in old Moynier's garden the flirt of skirts and the graceful reach of young round arms. Louis straightened himself on his crutches; he felt the stir and excitement of the game...he was divided between his old swagger and the pathetic droop of weakness...he swung slowly past the garden, and suddenly Suzon looked up...looked dully at first...with dawning recognition. Then she threw her apron over her face and shrieked, and fled into the house. There was something more than coquetry in the way she ran.

Louis turned into the lane and sat down under the black sage, he was not so strong as he had thought, and tried to be quite clear in his mind what this should mean. In a little while he was quite clear. Some children playing in the dust of the roadway at his approach had scuttled away like quail, and now he heard behind him the rustle of the sage, the intimation of hunched shoulders and fingers held over giggles of irrepressible excitement as they dared one another to come and peek at a fearsome thing.

It was that afternoon, when she came in with his soup and claret, that he asked Marguerita. The poor girl put down the bowl, and came and knelt by him very humble and gentle.

"Are you quite sure, Louis?" she asked, with her cheek upon his hand.

"I am sure of nothing," said he, "except that I cannot live without you."

It was very curious that no sooner had he said that than he began to discover it would be very hard to live with her; for to lose an ear and an eye and to have one's mouth drawn twisty by a scar does not make a kiss relish better if it falls not in with the natural desire.

Marguerita did not grow any prettier after she was married, but showed a tendency to take on fat, and she did not dress quite so well because she could not afford it, though there are times, as, for instance, when he has gone out in company and seen the young married women hustled out of sight of his scars, that her plain face looks almost good to him. Marguerita insists on their going out a great deal, to cock-fights and to *bàiles,* where he sits in the corner with his good side carefully disposed toward the guests, and his wife has given up dancing, though she is very fond of it, to sit beside him and keep him company; though, to tell the truth, Chabot could bear very well to do without that if only he could find himself surrounded by the lightness, the laughter, the half -revealing draperies, the delicious disputed moves of the game he loves - as he will not any more, for he knows now that such as these are not given save when there is something to be got by them, and though he is only thirty-four, poor Louis is no longer possessed of *l'art être désiré.*

For the rest of his life he will have to make the best of knowing that his wife carries his name with credit, and does not cost him anything. They are not without their comfortable hours. Marguerita takes excellent care of him, and she understands about sheep; if she sees the dust of a flock arising can tuck up her skirts and away to the edge of the town, getting back as much news of where they go, whence they come, and the conditions of the weather as Chabot could have brought himself, and not even her husband knows the extent of her devices for keeping him surrounded with the sense and stir of life. For it was not long after his marriage that Chabot made the discovery that all the quick desire of him toward lovely women warms in his wife's spirit toward the maimed and twisted thing that he is, and thwarted of the subtle play of lip and limb and eye, spends itself in offices of homely comfort.

And this is the bitterness of women which has come to him: that it matters not so much that they should have passion as the power to provoke it, and lacking the spark of a glance, the turn of an ankle, the treasures of tenderness in them wither unfulfilled. Shut behind his wife's fat, commonplace exterior lies the pulse of music, the delight of motion, the swimming sense, the quick, white burning fenced within his scars. Times like this he remembers what has passed between him and many women, and finds his complacency sicken and die in him. Knowing what he does of the state of her heart, and not being quite a cad, he does not make her an altogether bad husband, and if sometimes, looking at her with abhorring eyes - the shaking bosom, the arms enormous, the shade of her upper lip no longer to be mistaken for a smudge - resenting her lack of power to move him, he gives her a bad quarter of an hour, even there she has the best of him. For however unhappy he makes her, with one kiss of his crooked mouth he can set it all right again. But for Louis, the lift, the exultation, the exquisite, unmatched wonder of the world will not happen any more; never any more.

Chapter Thirteen - The House of Offence

IT began to be called the House when it was the only frame building in the camp, and wore its offence upon its front - long and low, little rooms, each with its own door opening upon the shallow veranda. Such a house in a mining country is the dial finger of prosperity. All the ores thereabout were argent, and as the lords of far market-places made silver to go up a few points, you were aware of it in the silken rustle and the heel-click of satin slippers in the House. When the Jews got their heads together and whispered in the Bourse, the gay skirts would flit and the lights go out in the little rooms behind the two cottonwood-trees that should have screened their entrances, but clacking their leaves as if forever fluttered and aghast at what went on in them, betrayed it all the more.

Inmates came and went; sometimes they had names and personalities, but mostly they were simply the women of the House. It was always spoken of in that way, as if but to pass the door-sill were to be seized of its full inheritance of turbulence and shame; and as the town poised and hung upon the turn of the appointed fortune of mining-camps, the House passed from being an outburst, an excess, to a backwater pool of enticement, wherein men swam or sunk themselves, and at last, as the quality of its attractions fell off with the grade of ores, it became merely the overt sign of an admitted and ineradicable baseness.

Always it served to keep alive in the camp the consciousness of style and the allurement of finery; for when the House was at its best, the conditions in desert camps, the price freight was, scrub-water to be bought by the gallon, the prohibitive cost of service, ground terribly the faces of good women. But they could always tell what kind of sleeves were being worn in San Francisco by watching the House. They all watched it; women whose lean breasts sagged from the lips of many children, virtuous slattern in calico, petted wives secure in a traditional honor; and their comment kept a stir about it like the pattering trail of the wind in the cottonwoods. In time, as the springs of mining interest drew away from that district to flash and rise again in some unguessed other side of the world, even that fell off before the dead weight of stable interests and a respectability too stale to be curious; the ground about it was parcelled off; all the accustomed activities of small towns went on around it screened from its contamination by no more than a high board fence, from which in time the palings rotted away. Good women exercised themselves no more against it than to prevent their children from playing under the shade of the two cottonwoods that broadened before it, like the shadow of professional impropriety, behind which the House had shrunk, and, in its condition of unregarded sordidness, pointed the last turn of the dial.

About this time it came into the sole possession of Hard Mag, who was handsome enough to have done much better by herself, and concerning whom nothing worth recording might have transpired had it not been for Mrs. Henby.

The Henbys had taken the place which faced the adjacent street and abutted on the back yard of the House. Henby was blast foreman at the Eclipse, and came home every other Sunday; and his wife, who was very fond of him, found a consolation for the lack of his company in the ordered life of the town. To wash on Monday, iron on Tuesday, bake on Wednesday, and keep the front room always looking as if nobody lived in it, gave Mrs. Henby a virtuous sense of well-being that she had not known in twenty years of scrambled existence at the mines. The trouble with Mrs. Henby was that she had no children. If there had been small footsteps going about the rooms and small finger-clutchings at her dress she would have been perfectly happy, and consequently had no time to trouble about the doing of the House. There had been hopes - but at forty, though her cheeks were smooth and bright, her hair still black, and her figure looking as if it had been melted and poured into her neat print wrapper, Mrs. Henby did not hope any more. She made a silk crazy-quilt for the bed-lounge in the parlor, and began to take an interest in Hard Mag and the draggled birds of passage that preened themselves occasionally in the dismantled rooms of the House, though being the most virtuous of women she would never have admitted the faintest distraction in the affairs of "such like."

It began by Mrs. Henby discovering, through the cracks of the fence, that Mag, in the intervals of sinning, was largely occupied with the tasks of widowed and neglected women. Mrs. Henby cut kindlings for herself sometimes if Henby was detained at the mine beyond his week-end visits, but to see Mag of the hard, red lips, the bright, unglinting hair, and the burnt-out blackness of her eyes under the pale, long lids, so employed made it of an amazing opprobriousness. For, as Mrs. Henby understood it, the root of sin lay in self-indulgence, and might be fostered by such small matters as sitting too much in rocking-chairs and wearing too becoming hats; she saw it now as the sign of an essential incompetency in the offices of creditable living. Mag, she perceived, did not even know how to pin up her skirts properly when she swept the back stoop. To see her thus fumbling at the mechanism of existence was to put her forever beyond the reach of resentment into the region of pitiable humanness. In time it grew upon Mrs. Henby that the poor creatures, who took the air of late afternoons in the yard behind the House, might have possibilities even of being interested in the crazy-quilt and the garden, and being prevented by some mysterious law of their profession from doing so. She went so far upon this supposition as to offer Mag a bunch of radishes out of her minute vegetable plot, which Mag, to her relief, refused. Mrs. Henby could no more refrain from neighborliness than she could help being large at the waist, but she really would not like to be seen handing things through the fence to the inmates of the House. She came to that in time, though.

Some wretched consort of Mag's fell sick at the House of the lead poisoning common in the mines when the doctor was away at Maverick, and nobody in the neighborhood so skilled in the remedies proper to the occasion as Mrs. Henby. This led to several conferences, and the passage between the palings of sundry preparations of hot milk and soups and custards. Mrs. Henby would hand them out after nightfall, and find the dishes on her side of the fence in the morning. She was so ashamed of it that she never told even her husband, and the man having gone away to his own place and died there, Mag had nobody to tell it to in any case. But Mrs. Henby always entertained a subconscious sureness that something unpleasant was likely to come of her condonings of inquity, and one morning, when she came out of the kitchen door to find Mag furtively waiting at the fence, she roughed forward all the quills of her respectability at once. Mag leaned her breast upon the point of a broken paling, as though the sharpness of it stayed her. She had no right to the desultory courtesies of back-fence neighborliness, and did not attempt them.

"I've had a letter," she said, abruptly, showing it clinched against her side; the knuckles of her hand were strained and white.

"A letter?"

"From Kansas. My daughter's coming." She lowered her voice and looked back cautiously at the shut House, as if the thing could overhear.

Well, You've Made Your Bed I Guess You Will Lie in It

So she had a daughter - this painted piece; and God-fearing women might long and long! Twenty years' resentment began to burn in Mrs. Henby's cushiony bosom.

"What are you doin' with a daughter?" she said.

"Oh," cried Mag, impatiently, "I had her years ago - ten - eleven years! She has been living with my aunt in Kansas: and now my aunt is dead, and they are sending her."

"Who is sending her?"

"I don't know - the neighbors. I've nobody belonging to me back there. They have to do something with her, so they are sending her to me. Here!" She struck upon the paling wickedly with her hand.

"Where's her father?" Mrs. Henby's interest rose superior to her resentment.

"How should I know? I tell you it was a long time ago. I came away when she was a little, little baby. My aunt was religious and couldn't have anything to do with me, but she took care of - her! I sent money."

Mrs. Henby recalled herself to the aloofness of entire respectability. "If your aunt wouldn't have you, I don't see how she could feel to abide your money?"

"I told her I was married," said Mag, "and respectable." She leaned upon the paling and laughed a hard, sharp laugh.

Mrs. Henby gathered up her apron full of kindlings.

"Well, you've made your bed," she said. "I guess you will lie in it."

But she sat down trembling as soon as she had shut the door. A daughter - to that woman - and she - Mrs. Henby went about shaking her head and talking to herself with indignation. All day the House remained shut and slumbering, its patched and unwashed windows staring blankly on the yard; but if ever Mrs. Henby came out of her kitchen door, as if she were the cuckoo on the striking of the hour, Mag appeared from the House. It was evident she had ordered a clear field for herself, for no one came out in draggled finery to take the air that day. It was dusk before Mrs. Henby's humanness got the better of her. She went out to the wood-pile and whispered to the stirring of Mag's dress:

"When's she coming?"

"Wednesday. She will be started before I can get a letter to her."

"Well, I reckon you'll have to take her," said Mrs. Henby, unconsolingly. A flash of Mag's insuperable hardness broke from her.

"She'll spoil trade," she said.

Mrs. Henby looked up the dusky bulk of the House beyond her, lines of light at the windows like the red lids of distempered eyes. All at once, and, as she said afterward, without for the moment any consciousness relativity, she recalled the quagmires of unwarned waterholes where cattle sink and flounder, and the choking call of warning that sounds to the last above the stifling slime. When Mag said that about the child and her way of making a living, Mrs. Henby jumped. She thought she heard the smothering suck of the mire. Somebody in the House laughed and cried out coarsely, and then she heard Mag's voice going on hurriedly behind the palings:

"Mrs. Henby! Mrs. Henby! you've got to help me - I must find some place for her to board - She has been well brought up, I tell you. My aunt is religious - She would be a comfort to some good person."

"Meaning me, I suppose," sniffed Mrs. Henby. Mag had not meant anybody in particular, but she swept it up urgently.

"Oh, if you would she'd be a comfort to you! She's real sweet-looking - they sent me her picture once." She felt for phrases to touch the other woman, but they rang insincerely. "You'd be the saving of her - if you would."

"Well, I won't!" snapped Mrs. Henby; and as soon as she was inside she locked the door against even the suggestion. "Me to take anything off that painted piece!" she quivered, angrily.

It was five days until Wednesday, and Mag struck to her trail insistently.

"You been thinking of what I said last night?" she questioned in the morning interval at the woodpile.

Mrs. Henby denied it, but she had. She had thought of what Henby would say to it, and wondered if Mag's daughter had hard eyes, and bright, unglinting, canary-colored hair. She thought of what explanation she might make to the neighbors in case she decided suddenly to adopt the daughter of – of an old friend in Kansas; then she thought of the faces of the women who went in and out of the House, and resolved not to think any more.

She kept away from the woodpile as much as possible during Saturday and Sunday, but Monday evening she heard Mag calling her from the back of the yard. This was the worst yet, for there was no telling who might overhear.

"Mrs. Henby," demanded the painted piece, "are you going to see that innocent child brought to this place and never lift a hand to it?"

"I don't know as I got any call to interfere," said Mrs. Henby.

"And you with a good home, and calling yourself Christian, and all," went on the hard one. "Besides, I'd pay you."

"I don't feel to need any of your money," thrust in Mrs. Henby, resentfully. "I guess I could take care of one child without - but I ain't going to." She broke off, and moved rapidly toward the house.

"Mrs. Henby, listen to me!" cried Mag, shaking at the palings as though they had been the bars of a cage and she trapped in it. "For God's sake, Mrs. Henby, you must! Mrs. Henby, if you won't listen to me here, I shall come to your house."

Mrs. Henby heard the crack of the rotten palings as she shut the door.

"Mrs. Henby! Mrs. Henby!" threatened the voice, "I'm coming in!"

Then the crash of splintering wood, and Mag's hand on the knob. The vehemence of her mood, her tragic movements, the bright vividness of her lips and hair seemed to force Mrs. Henby into the attitude of the offender. She sat limply in a chair twisting her hands in her fat lap while the other assailed her. Behind her on the wall Mag's shadow shook and threatened like the shape of an uncouth destiny.

"I know what you are thinking, Mrs. Henby. You think there's bad blood, and she will turn out like me maybe, but I tell you it's no such thing. Look here - if it's any satisfaction to you to know - I was good when I had her, and her father was good - only we were young and didn't know any better - we hadn't any feelings except what we'd have had if we had been married - only we didn't happen to - It's the truth, Mrs. Henby, if I die for it. Bad blood!" she said, hardness augmenting upon her. "How many a man comes to the House and goes away to raise a family, and not a word said about bad blood! You don't reckon -"

But Mrs. Henby had her apron over her face, and was crying into it. Mag floundered back to the other woman's point of view.

"If it is a question what she'll come to, you know well enough if I have to take her with me. *Me!*" she said. She threw round herself an indescribable air of lascivious deviltry, as though she had been blown upon by the blast of an unseen furnace, and the shadow upon the wall shook and confirmed it, "That's what she will come to unless you save her from it. It's up to you, Mrs. Henby."

"I - I don't know what Henby will say," whimpered Mrs. Henby, afresh.

"Say?" urged Mag, with the scorn of her kind for the well-regulated husband. "He'll say anything he thinks you want him to say. He'll be as fond as anything of her - and you can bring her up to be a comfort to him." The poverty of Mag's experience furnished him with no phrases to express what a child might become.

"A nice time I'd have," burst out the other woman, in a last throb of resentment, "bringing her up to be a comfort to anybody, with her own mother living a sinful life right under her eyes."

"Oh," said Mag, with enlightenment, "so that's what is troubling you! Well - if you say the word - I'll clear out. The girls will kick - but they have to do what I say. Look here, then! If you'll take the kid - I'll go."

"And never come back nor let her know?"

"Cross my heart to die," said Mag.

"Well, then" - Mrs. Henby let her apron fall tremulously - "I'll take her."

"For keeps?"

"For keeps," vowed Mrs. Henby, solemnly.

They were silent, regarding each other for a time, neither knowing how to terminate the interview without offence.

"What's her name?" asked Mrs. Henby, timidly, at last.

"Marietta."

Mag searched her scant remembrances and brought up this: "She's got dark hair."

Mrs. Henby was visibly comforted.

Mrs. Henby found, after all, that she was not put to any great strain of inventiveness to account for the little girl she had decided to adopt, the event being overshadowed, in the estimation of the townspeople, by the more memorable one which occurred on the very night of Marietta's arrival. This was no less than the departure of Hard Mag and the women of the House. They went out of it as they came, with scant warning, helped by coarse laughter of the creatures they had preyed upon, and with so much of careless haste that about two hours after their flitting - caught, it was supposed, from their neglected fires - the whole shell of the House burst into flame. It made a red flare in the windows in the middle of the night, but, as none of the townspeople had any interest in it and no property was endangered, it was allowed to burn quite out, which it did as quickly as the passions it had thrived upon, to an inconsiderable heap of cinders. The next year the Henbys took over the place where it had stood for a garden, and Henby made a swing under the cottonwood-trees for his adopted daughter.

Chapter Fourteen - The Walking Woman

THE first time of my hearing of her was at Temblor. We had come all one day between blunt, whitish bluffs rising from mirage water, with a thick, pale wake of dust billowing from the wheels, all the dead wall of the foothills sliding and shimmering with heat, to learn that the Walking Woman had passed us somewhere in the dizzying dimness, going down to the Tulares on her own feet. We heard of her again in the Carrisal, and again at Adobe Station, where she had passed a week before the shearing, and at last I had a glimpse of her at the Eighteen-Mile House as I went hurriedly northward on the Mojave stage; and afterward sheepherders at whose camps she slept, and cowboys at rodeos, told me as much of her way of life as they could understand. Like enough they told her as much of mine. That was very little. She was the Walking Woman, and no one knew her name, but because she was a sort of whom men speak respectfully, they called her to her face Mrs. Walker, and she answered to it if she was so inclined. She came and went about our western world on no discoverable errand, and whether she had some place of refuge where she lay by in the interim, or whether between her seldom, unaccountable appearances in our quarter she went on steadily walking, was never learned. She came and went, oftenest in a kind of muse of travel which the untrammelled space begets, or at rare intervals flooding wondrously with talk, never of herself, but of things she had known and seen. She must have seen some rare happenings, too - by report. She was at Maverick the time of the Big Snow, and at Tres Piños when they brought home the body of Morena; and if anybody could have told whether De Borba killed Mariana for spite or defence, it would have been she, only she could not be found when most wanted. She was at Tunawai at the time of the cloud-burst, and if she had cared for it could have known most desirable things of the ways of trail-making, burrow-habiting small things.

All of which should have made her worth meeting, though it was not, in fact, for such things I was wishful to meet her; and as it turned out, it was not of these things we talked when at last we came together. For one thing, she was a woman, not old, who had gone about alone in a country where the number of women is as one in fifteen. She had eaten and slept at the herder's camps, and laid by for days at one-man stations whose masters had no other touch of human kind than the passing of chance prospectors, or the halting of the tri-weekly stage. She had been set on her way by teamsters who lifted her out of white, hot desertness and put her down at the crossing of unnamed ways, days distant from anywhere. And through all this she passed unarmed and unoffended. I had the best testimony to this, the witness of the men themselves. I think they talked of it because they were so much surprised at it. It was not, on the whole, what they expected of themselves.

Well I understand that nature which wastes its borders with too eager burning, beyond which rim of desolation it flares forever quick and white, and have had some inkling of the isolating calm of a desire too high to stoop to satisfaction. But you could not think of these things pertaining to the Walking Woman; and if there were ever any truth in the exemption from offence residing in a frame of behavior called ladylike, it should have been inoperative here. What this really means is that you get no affront so long as your behavior in the estimate of the particular audience invites none. In the estimate of the immediate audience - conduct which affords protection in Mayfair gets you no consideration in Maverick. And by no cañon could it be considered ladylike to go about on your own feet, with a blanket and a black bag and almost no money in your purse, in and about the haunts of rude and solitary men.

There were other things that pointed the wish for a personal encounter with the Walking Woman. One of them was the contradiction of reports of her - as to whether she was comely, for example. Report said yes, and again, plain to the point of deformity. She had a twist to her face, some said; a hitch to one shoulder; they averred she limped as she walked. But by the distance she covered she should have been straight and young. As to sanity, equal incertitude. On the mere evidence of her way of life she was cracked; not quite broken, but unserviceable. Yet in her talk there was both wisdom and information, and the word she brought about trails and water-holes was as reliable as an Indian's.

By her own account she had begun by walking off an illness. There had been an invalid to be taken care of for years, leaving her at last broken in body, and with no recourse but her own feet to carry her out of that predicament. It seemed there had been, besides the death of her invalid, some other worrying affairs, upon which, and the nature of her illness, she was never quite clear, so that it might very well have been an un-soundness of mind which drove her to the open, sobered and healed at last by the large soundness of nature. It must have been about that time that she lost her name. I am convinced that she never told it because she did not know it herself. She was the Walking Woman, and the country people called her Mrs. Walker. At the time I knew her, though she wore short hair and a man's boots, and had a fine down over all her face from exposure to the weather, she was perfectly sweet and sane.

I had met her occasionally at ranch-houses and road-stations, and had got as much acquaintance as the place allowed; but for the things I wished to know there wanted a time of leisure and isolation. And when the occasion came we talked altogether of other things.

It was at Warm Spring in the Little Antelope I came upon her in the heart of a clear forenoon. The spring lies off a mile from the main trail, and has the only trees about it known in that country. First you come up-on a pool of waste full of weeds of a poisonous dark green, every reed ringed about the water-level with a muddy white incrustation. Then the three oaks appear staggering on the slope, and the spring sobs and blub-bers below them in ashy-colored mud. All the hills of that country have the down plunge toward the desert and back abruptly toward the Sierra. The grass is thick and brittle and bleached straw-color toward the end of the season. As I rode up the swale of the spring I saw the Walking Woman sitting where the grass was deepest, with her black bag and blanket, which she carried on a stick, beside her. It was one of those days when the genius of talk flows as smoothly as the rivers of mirage through the blue hot desert morning.

You are not to suppose that in my report of a Borderer I give you the words only, but the full meaning of the speech. Very often the words are merely the punctuation of thought; rather, the crests of the long waves of intercommunicative silences. Yet the speech of the Walking Woman was fuller than most.

The best of our talk that day began in some dropped word of hers from which I inferred that she had had a child. I was surprised at that, and then wondered why I should have been surprised, for it is the most natural of all experiences to have children. I said something of that purport, and al-so that it was one of the perquisites of living I should be least willing to do without. And that led to the Walking Woman saying that there were three things which if you had known you could cut out all the rest, and they were good any way you got them, but best if, as in her case, they were related to and grew each one out of the others. It was while she talked that I decided that she really did have a twist to her face, a sort of natural warp or skew into which it fell when it was worn merely as a countenance, but which disappeared the moment it became the vehicle of thought or feeling.

The first of the experiences the Walking Woman had found most worthwhile had come to her in a sand-storm on the south slope of Tehachapi in a dateless spring. I judged it should have been about the time she began to find herself, after the period of worry and loss in which her wandering began. She had come, in a day pricked full of intimations of a storm, to the camp of Filon Geraud, whose companion shepherd had gone a three days' *pasear* to Mojave for supplies. Geraud was of great hardihood, red-blooded, of a full laughing eye, and an indubitable spark for women. It was the season of the year when there is a soft bloom on the days, but the nights are cowering cold and the lambs tender, not yet flockwise. At such times a sand-storm works incalculable disaster. The lift of the wind is so great that the whole surface of the ground appears to travel upon it slantwise, thinning out miles high in air. In the intolerable smother the lambs are lost from the ewes; neither dogs nor man make headway against it.

The morning flared through a horizon of yellow smudge, and by midforenoon the flock broke.

"There were but the two of us to deal with the trouble," said the Walking Woman. "Until that time I had not known how strong I was, nor how good it is to run when running is worth while. The flock travelled down the wind, the sand bit our faces; we called, and after a time heard the words broken and beaten small by the wind. But after a little we had not to call. All the time of our running in the yellow dusk of day and the black dark of night, I knew where Filon was. A flock-length away, I knew him. Feel? What should I feel? I knew. I ran with the flock and turned it this way and that as Filon would have.

"Such was the force of the wind that when we came together we held by one another and talked a little between pantings. We snatched and ate what we could as we ran. All that day and night until the next afternoon the camp kit was not out of the cayaques. But we held the flock. We herded them under a butte when the wind fell off a little, and the lambs sucked; when the storm rose they broke, but we kept upon their track and brought them together again. At night the wind quieted, and we slept by turns; at least Filon slept. I lay on the ground when my turn was and beat with the storm. I was no more tired than the earth was. The sand filled in the creases of the blanket, and where I turned, dripped back upon the ground. But we saved the sheep. Some ewes there were that would not give down their milk because of the worry of the storm, and the lambs died. But we kept the flock together. And I was not tired."

The Walking Woman stretched out her arms and clasped herself, rocking in them as if she would have hugged the recollection to her breast.

"For you see," said she, "I worked with a man, without excusing, without any burden on me of looking or seeming. Not fiddling or fumbling as women work, and hoping it will all turn out for the best. It was not for Filon to ask, Can you, or Will you. He said, Do, and I did. And my work was good. We held the flock. And that," said the Walking Woman, the t ist coming in her face again, "is one of the things that make you able to do without the others."

"Yes," I said; and then, "What others?"

"Oh," she said, as if it pricked her, "the looking and the seeming."

And I had not thought until that time that one who had the courage to be the Walking Woman would have cared! We sat and looked at the pattern of the thick crushed grass on the slope, wavering in the fierce noon like the waterings in the coat of a tranquil beast; the ache of a world-old bitterness sobbed and whispered in the spring. At last -

"It is by the looking and the seeming," said I, "that the opportunity finds you out."

"Filon found out," said the Walking Woman. She smiled; and went on from that to tell me how, when the wind went down about four o'clock and left the afternoon clear and tender, the flock began to feed, and they had out the kit from the cayaques, and cooked a meal. When it was over, and Filon had his pipe between his teeth, he came over from his side of the fire, of his own notion, and stretched himself on the ground beside her. Of his own notion. There was that in the way she said it that made it seem as if nothing of the sort had happened before to the Walking Woman, and for a moment I thought she was about to tell me one of the things I wished to know; but she went on to say what Filon had said to her of her work with the flock. Obvious, kindly things, such as any man in sheer decency would have said, so that there must have something more gone with the words to make them so treasured of the Walking Woman.

"We were very comfortable," said she, "and not so tired as we expected to be. Filon leaned up on his elbow. I had not noticed until then how broad he was in the shoulders, and how strong in the arms. And we had saved the flock together. We felt that. There was something that said together, in the slope of his shoulders toward me. It was around his mouth and on the cheek high up under the shine of his eyes. And under the shine the look - the look that said, 'We are of one sort and one mind' - his eyes that were the color of the flat water in the toulares - do you know the look?"

"I know it."

"The wind was stopped and all the earth smelled of dust, and Filon understood very well that what I had done with him I could not have done so well with another. And the look - the look in the eyes -"

"Ah-ah -!"

I have always said, I will say again, I do not know why at this point the Walking Woman touched me. If it were merely a response to my unconscious throb of sympathy, or the unpremeditated way of her heart to declare that this, after all, was the best of all indispensable experiences; or if in some flash of forward vision, encompassing the unimpassioned years, the stir, the movement of tenderness were for *me* - but no; as often as I have thought of it, I have thought of a different reason, but no conclusive one, why the Walking Woman should have put out her hand and laid it on my arm.

"To work together, to love together," said the Walking Woman, withdrawing her hand again; "there you have two of the things; the other you know."

"The mouth at the breast," said I.

"The lips and the hands," said the Walking Woman. "The little, pushing hands and the small cry." There ensued a pause of fullest understanding, while the land before us swam in the noon, and a dove in the oaks behind the spring began to call. A little red fox came out of the hills and lapped delicately at the pool.

"I stayed with Filon until the fall," said she. "All that summer in the Sierras, until it was time to turn south on the trail. It was a good time, and longer than he could be expected to have loved one like me. And besides, I was no longer able to keep the trail. My baby was born in October."

Whatever more there was to say to this, the Walking Woman's hand said it, straying with remembering gesture to her breast. There are so many ways of loving and working, but only one way of the first-born. She added after an interval, that she did not know if she would have given up her walking to keep at home and tend him, or whether the thought of her son's small feet running beside her in the trails would have driven her to the open again. The baby had not stayed long enough for that. "And whenever the wind blows in the night," said the Walking Woman, "I wake and wonder if he is well covered."

She took up her black bag and her blanket; there was the ranch-house of Dos Palos to be made before night, and she went as outliers do, without a hope expressed of another meeting and no word of good-bye. She was the Walking Woman. That was it. She had walked off all sense of society-made values, and, knowing the best when the best came to her, was able to take it. Work - as I believed; love - as the Walking Woman had proved it; a child - as you subscribe to it. But look you: it was the naked thing the

Walking Woman grasped, not dressed and tricked out, for instance, by prejudices in favor of certain occupations; and love, man love, taken as it came, not picked over and rejected if it carried no obligation of permanency; and a child; *any* way you get it, a child is good to have, say nature and the Walking Woman; to have it and not to wait upon a proper concurrence of so many decorations that the event may not come at all.

At least one of us is wrong. To work and to love and to bear children. *That* sounds easy enough. But the way we live establishes so many things of much more importance.

Far down the dim, hot valley I could see the Walking Woman with her blanket and black bag over her shoulder. She had a queer, sidelong gait, as if in fact she had a twist all through her.

Recollecting suddenly that people called her lame, I ran down to the open place below the spring where she had passed. There in the bare, hot sand the track of her two feet bore evenly and white.

www.ingramcontent.com/pod-product-compliance
Lightning Source LLC
Chambersburg PA
CBHW051846040426
42447CB00006B/726